Guide to Teaching the Early Grades

Oak Meadow

Oak Meadow, Inc.
Post Office Box 615
Putney, Vermont 05346
oakmeadow.com

ISBN 978-1-68427-001-9
Item #b000005
v.030822

Table of Contents

Introduction vii

Learning Processes 1

Elements of Successful Learning Processes.. 1

Facilitating the Learning Process 2

Learning through Imaginative Play 6

    Creative Play 6

    Sand and Water Play 7

The Art of Storytelling 9

Choosing Stories... 10

Telling the Story.. 11

Developing Your Voice... 12

Creating Stories 13

    Creating a Story to Be Told Later... 15

    Creating a Story Spontaneously.. 16

Nature Stories 17

Archetypal Stories... 19

The Importance of Fairy Tales... 20

Art Instruction 23

Crayon Drawing 23

Tips on Teaching a Child to Draw.. 24

Drawing Forth Your Own Inner Artist 27

Form Drawing 28

Basic Types of Form Drawing.. 28

Watercolor Painting 32

Wet-Paper Painting 32

Working with Color 34

The Painting Process 34

Clay Sculpting 35

Tips for Working with Clay 36

Creating Form out of Clay 37

Guidelines for Handcrafting 39

Using Color in a Purposeful Way 39

Finger Knitting 40

Knitting... 42

Knitting Instructions.. 43

First Knitting Projects 48

Crocheting... 49

Music Instruction 55

Singing 55
Choosing Songs for Children 55
Guiding Music Time Activities 56
Singing Tips 57

Playing the Recorder 58
Tips on Teaching the Recorder 59

Appendix 61

Tongue Twisters and Letter Rhymes 63

Songs, Verses, and Fingerplays 69
Opening Verses for Circle Time 69
Closing Verses for Circle Time 70

Poems 121
Poems by Maud Keary 121
Poems by Edward Lear 136
Poems by Dollie Radford 140
Poems by Robert Louis Stevenson 147

Verses and Poems Especially for Grade 3 159

List of Songs, Verses, Fingerplays, and Poems 171
Verses in Alphabetical Order 171
Poems 173
Verses and Poems Especially for Grade 3 175

Introduction

Homeschooling is a journey for the parent as much as for the child. The main requirement is a willingness to learn together (and maybe a dose of courage!). However, many parents approach homeschooling with very little, if any, teaching experience. Some parents can feel uncertain about what to do and may worry that if they don't do something "right," their child will suffer. After decades of working with homeschooling families, we can assure you that if you are willing to learn and keep your love for your child as the focus of your intentions, you are almost certain to succeed.

The art of teaching is a noble art and one to which many people dedicate their lives. Even if you have never taught other children, you have been teaching your children since they were born. Your parenting instincts can help guide you in your teaching. Because you know your child best, you will be able to use your innate sensitivity to your child's needs to help you shape and customize your learning activities.

Oak Meadow Guide to Teaching the Early Grades is designed to give you some important information about the learning process and the art of teaching. We've drawn on the vast and varied experience of Oak Meadow's teachers in creating this guide, and we hope it provides you the support you need to become a confident, effective home teacher. You are encouraged to read this book before you begin teaching and to refer to it often throughout your homeschooling years. As you become more experienced as a teacher, you will be able to more fully use and expand on the information here. You will find Oak Meadow's *The Heart of Learning* to be another essential resource in your development as a teacher.

Above all, remember to enjoy this incredible time with your children. Learning is an exciting process of discovery for both teacher and student. By sharing a natural curiosity and love of learning with your children, you will have a rich and wondrous educational journey.

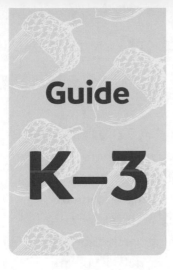

Learning Processes

Learning is a process, and facilitating this process is what the art of teaching is all about. There are many activities we can offer children that support a rich learning experience. These activities don't have to be elaborate, though—even the simplest activity can be used in a learning process. It is the amount of life you bring to the activity that determines the depth of experience you will have together.

As teachers, we may not always feel filled with life and energy, and in those cases we must consider what kinds of activities actually have the ability to draw us into a deeper experience, even when we're not feeling up to it. Some activities seem, by their very nature, to thwart the very possibility of deeper experience. Others seem to have the power to inspire and delight while bringing us into a fuller sense of our potential.

Elements of Successful Learning Processes

How can we determine which activities will support the learning process best? There are several elements that are common to activities that provide opportunities for deeper expression. Some activities have all of these elements, while others have only one or two. An activity does not necessarily have to have all three of these elements, but for an activity to offer real opportunities for deeper expression, it must have at least one of these elements present:

The Activity Is Rhythmical

This should be understood in a broad sense, and does not mean the activity must have drums beating in the background, or involve singing, clapping, or dancing (although it might!). Rhythm has to do with the repetition of a particular motion numerous times, eventually resulting in a finished activity. This includes such activities as knitting, sewing, weaving, form drawing, singing rounds, and folk dancing. Reciting the times tables can be a rhythmic activity, as can reading poetry aloud, if it has a clear, repetitive meter and rhyming scheme. The repetition of a particular action creates an opportunity for focus that is not available in other, more erratic activities where the mind is constantly making decisions. It provides the mind and body with an activity that is steady, consistent, and nonthreatening (because it is familiar). Once we are able to relax our minds in this way, we can open to the experience of process.

The Activity Is Creative

This includes such activities as clay sculpting, woodworking, painting, and drawing, as well as any activity that allows you to use the imagination to create something. In creative activities, there is a flexible medium present that allows the child to give form to an inner impulse. These activities encourage strong connection between your child's physical being and the inner creative nature and innate abilities. The particular medium used in the creative process influences the nature of the experience. In general, materials that are softer and more malleable are preferred over anything harsh or brittle, and it is usually preferable to choose a natural material over a synthetic one. For example, if you are doing a sculpting project, clay would be better than commercial Play-Doh. If you are drawing, crayons generally encourage a freer form of expression than markers. Natural colors are more conducive to a reflective experience than "day-glo" colors, and wood has a richer feel than plastic.

The Activity Embodies Archetypes

We'll talk in greater detail about archetypes in the storytelling section of this guide, but essentially, the basic concept is that all physical forms and activities are reflections of deeper realities. If an activity incorporates or embodies archetypes, that activity has the power to help those who are involved (children and adults) to transcend their limiting emotional and mental patterns. This lets them begin to experience the deeper movements of life, opening them up to expressing their natural capacity for intelligence and loving concern for others. Although archetypal symbols can appear in many activities, the activity in which this can occur most clearly and strongly is storytelling.

These are some of the fundamental elements that comprise effective, beneficial learning processes, and should be considered before you begin an activity.

Facilitating the Learning Process

As you prepare to enter into a specific learning process with your child, we suggest reflecting on the following areas so that you can feel confident in your approach. These guidelines are based on the experiences of many teachers over many years. If you feel unsure about what you are doing, they can be a helpful tool for getting started. However, as you progress in your understanding of the elements involved, you will begin to rely less on formal guidelines and more on your own perceptions.

If things do not go according to plan, don't worry! Just stop doing whatever it is you are doing, relax, reestablish the relationship between you and your child, and then decide whether you want to continue with the process, or move on to something else. As you reflect later on the experience, review in your mind the sequence of events and see where you might have done something differently. Then, let it go and get ready for the next day's learning processes.

Here are the guidelines for entering into an effective, satisfying learning process:

Clear Your Time and Space

In order to be able to enter fully into the experience of a learning process, we must first develop our capacity to focus. This is not as simple as it might seem. In the course of our daily affairs, there are many elements that arise that demand our attention. Minimizing interruptions can help you remain focused on the learning process at hand. As you increase your ability to focus, you will become better able to maintain your focus in the midst of your activities.

The following points can be very helpful in clearing a time and space for you to engage in the learning process:

a. Keep a daily to-do list. This relieves your mind of the pressure of remembering "all those things I must do." Once you schedule all that needs to be accomplished in the day or week, then you are more able to focus on what you are doing now.

b. Put away your phone and other electronic devices while you are engaged in teaching. This is absolutely essential, especially in a busy household. You must be very clear that, for the duration of the process, you will not be available to anyone but your child.

c. Put a note on your door: "Do Not Disturb Until (time)." Inform your friends and neighbors that you are busy during certain hours. It helps to do this at the same time every day so that people get used to the idea and plan to visit or call at other times.

d. Make sure that the space you are using is clean and orderly. A confused space makes a confused mind.

e. Gather together all the materials that you will need ahead of time. Lay out all of the materials in an organized way so that you are certain you haven't forgotten anything.

f. Once the environment has been prepared, take a minute to relax and center yourself on the work ahead. When you are centered and poised, sit down together with your child to begin the learning process.

Take into Account Younger Siblings

If you have younger children, explain to them that you have some important work to do, and that you and your older child cannot be interrupted during this time. At the same time, offer them a special activity of their own to do while you are teaching.

Be very clear, in your own mind, about the importance of this focused time with your child. If you have an infant, you will obviously have to schedule things around the baby's nap time or when you can have someone available to help you.

Young children are quite capable of adapting to a routine and will be more willing to give you the necessary time if you are consistent in your time. For example, if your children can expect that they will eat breakfast and go for a walk most days, and then return home to draw or play with certain toys while you and your older child "do school," the young ones will understand and cooperate with this routine. Teaching young children that there are times you shouldn't be disturbed has to be done with loving patience. It may take a week or more to get your younger children used to spending time alone without calling for your attention, but the time spent cultivating this will be well worth it.

Nurture the Teacher/Student Relationship

The most important aspect of any learning process is the relationship that you have with the other person. Your primary focus as a teacher should be staying alert to the needs of the student. As you develop your capacity to focus and respond to their needs in the midst of the learning process, you will not need any guidelines, techniques, or approaches. You will naturally unfold your own unique approach, and will learn how to respond more sensitively to the needs of the student in each moment. At that point, your only work will be to remain focused so that you can respond to these needs.

Each time you and your child begin work, take a few moments to reconnect. This may mean talking briefly about something that is familiar, or looking at something interesting in the immediate environment. This is the expansive phase of the process, before you focus on the work at hand, so just keep it light and undemanding.

Start with Something Simple and Familiar

A good way to begin a new learning process is to review things that were covered in the last session. This helps establish a common ground and brings to mind the foundation on which the new material rests. The review is a chance to appreciate the child's progress in learning. The expansive, comfortable, confident feeling still infuses this stage of the process.

Make a Transition into the Unfamiliar

This is the beginning of the next phase of the learning process and can be the most difficult for teachers. It begins when you feel that you and the other person have established a good relationship, and after you have experienced the "simple and familiar" stage for several minutes. The shift from the previous stage to this one occurs gradually, so there are no absolute rules that determine when this happens, but if you are watching closely you can usually detect an opening that allows you to move smoothly into this stage.

When the child feels confident with the material being reviewed, they will feel present and involved in what is occurring. When the child first moves into the unfamiliar territory of material that has not been fully grasped, it is common for their presence to momentarily wane; you will sense an uncertainty. This is the opportunity for learning.

Engaging the Learning Process

When working on familiar skills that are still being developed, always take the time to notice ways in which your child has succeeded. If, for instance, your child is playing a song on the recorder, and they falter in the middle and become uncertain, just encourage your child to continue. Afterward, congratulate your child on how well the tune was played, but mention that there was just one part that was not quite right. Even if there were seven parts not right, just mention one. After that point has been worked on, you can easily go to another, and another, but to say that there were seven parts that were wrong can have an overwhelming effect. Point out the error that was made, and model the correct method for your child.

This applies to any subject, and any activity. If your child is doing long division, and gets stuck and uncertain partway through, help them keep going, and then afterward look at one element that will help the process flow more smoothly the next time. If your child is reading aloud, use your own confident presence to encourage them to continue, even if some words are stumbled over. Afterward, comment on the lovely expressive tone or diction, and then look at the tricky word and find ways to decode it, and others like it. If your child is recording data on a chart for science and seems confused by the procedure, simply give support as needed, focusing first on what your child is doing right, and then looking at how to clarify an element that is making the task seem too difficult.

At this point, the most important element is your attitude. Pointing out and correcting an error should not be done with a critical voice. Instead, proceed as if sharing interesting information about something you're doing together. After you have given instruction, work with the material a few times until your child seems to be clear about it, or begins to lose interest in doing it correctly. At that point, it is probably time to move on.

Remember, you're not doing this to force your child to learn—you're in this to share the enjoyment of the learning process. If the process stops being enjoyable, learning has probably stopped taking place. Let it go and come back to it another day.

Introduce New Material

After you have played with skills development in the context of familiar material, and if things are still progressing in a positive way, then you can begin to share new material.

Introduce the new material as clearly as possible, but don't be concerned about whether your child is immediately interested in it. Just present it as something that might be fun to learn or do. If your child's interest is caught, then break it up into parts to keep the learning manageable. When all of the pieces of the new material are learned, join them together one by one, showing how they are connected.

Some children prefer to learn new material as one whole unit, so feel free to respond to the needs of your child. After working with the new material (in whole or in parts) for a bit, you can put it aside for the day. Your child will continue to absorb the material throughout the day and even while sleeping. When you review the material in a day or so, you can add a new piece.

Reflect on the Learning Process

After the learning process is finished or at the end of the day, sit down by yourself and review the events that occurred. If you had trouble during the process, review in your mind what happened and try to see where things went wrong. Perhaps you could find ways to incorporate rhythmic, creative, or archetypal elements to help bring the learning process to life. Depending on your child, you may want to discuss what went wrong and how it might have happened differently. Above all, don't blame anyone, especially yourself. Just learn from your experiences, let it go, and get ready for the next day's learning experience.

There have been wonderful new explorations and discoveries into different styles of learning in children. Learning styles are discussed in depth in Oak Meadow's *The Heart of Learning*, and we encourage you to consider the different ways children learn as it may inform your individual approach to learning processes. If you are interested in additional resources about learning processes and learning styles, some wonderful references for the study of the development of young children are *Magical Child*, *The Crack in the Cosmic Egg*, and *Evolution's End*, all by Joseph Chilton-Pearce. He does an excellent job describing developmental phases of young children with an emphasis on preserving the wonder and innocence of childhood.

Learning through Imaginative Play

A child's imagination can provide endless opportunities for learning and enjoyment. Usually all it takes is to provide your child with a few basic tools and simple materials, and you will find that they begin exploring imaginatively without additional effort on your part.

If your child is having trouble getting started playing, it is fine to casually remember a story you shared or a topic of interest that you have been learning about. By creating an image of something familiar, you are giving your child a spark to begin their own imaginative process. Soon your child will begin to build play around the familiar image, but there is no end to where the imagination can go from there. (For more on imaginative play, see *The Heart of Learning*.)

Creative Play

Creative play often becomes an extension of the focused lesson time. It is a rich and rewarding way for children to integrate their knowledge and experiences. Creative play requires very few props. In fact, it seems that the more "stuff" a child has surrounding them, the more likely we are to hear cries of, "I'm bored! I don't have anything to do!" Too much stuff can make individual toys inaccessible.

Taking some time to organize what is available to your child, and rotating toys so that there is a manageable selection, can enhance your child's creative play. Have a "50 percent reduction" day and store half of everything. Do you have five puzzles out? Put away two or three for now. Do you have a dozen stuffed animals in an overflowing basket? Choose six to keep and six to take a break ("take a vacation"). Clearing out and bringing order to the physical spaces of play and learning can have a positive, refreshing influence on children and parents alike.

Creative activities should be included in each day simply for pure entertainment and enjoyment (their built-in educational value is just a bonus!):

- Drawing
- Painting

- Craft projects

- Making music

- Singing

- Dancing

- Plays and puppet shows

- Woodworking

- Cooking

- Obstacle courses

- Scavenger hunts

- Treasure hunts

- Fort building (indoors or outside)

- Outdoor explorations of all kinds

Sand and Water Play

Sand and water play are incredibly satisfying sensory experiences that encourage hours of creative fun.

Sand play offers many wonderful opportunities to budding scientists. You only need a pile of sand and some natural materials such as branches, leaves, small sticks, stones, acorns or other seed pods, grass, etc. Variations for playing with sand may include using containers of different sizes and shapes, small play figures (such as animals), and a small pail of water. Your child can make mountains, rivers, and little landscapes.

A "drip castle" can be made by mixing a soggy mixture of water and sand, scooping small handfuls of it up, and then allowing it to drop down into a pile, adding bit by bit up into an unusual "castle." The water dries out fairly quickly, keeping the sand usable.

If you don't have a sandbox, we strongly recommend building one. It can provide hours of beneficial imaginative play, and it is relatively easy to make.

To make a sandbox: Four 1" x 12" x 6' boards work well. Nail the four boards together (end to end) into the shape of a square, and place them on the ground. If you want, you can dig a small trench (about 3"–4" deep would be sufficient) the same size as the square and fit the boards into it. This will keep it from losing its shape and will also help to keep the sand from slipping under the boards. You may also want to brace the corners. When it is in place, fill the enclosed area with several bags of clean sand, which is available at most building supply stores.

If you live in an apartment or for some other reason aren't able to make a permanent outdoor sandbox, you can still make a smaller, portable version using a plastic tray of the type that is used for kitty litter.

These are sold in grocery stores or pet shops. There are also commercially available plastic sandboxes with lids that can be used to prevent animals from getting into the sand.

Another sensory experience that is beneficial for young children is water play. This is a very simple activity, but it provides hours of enjoyment. It is best done outdoors and requires very little preparation. If you live in a cold climate, this could be done in the bathtub or at the sink.

Dress your child (and yourself) in old clothes, or a bathing suit, if weather permits. Gather together an assortment of containers. These can be pots, pans, bottles, old dish soap squirt bottles, buckets, cups, etc.—anything that can hold water (but nothing glass, as that can easily break). The wider the variety of containers, the better it is. Include several different sizes of spoons and scoops (old laundry soap scoops work well), and consider poking different sizes of holes in a few of the plastic containers.

Then, set up an old table outdoors and put all of the containers on the table. Next, fill the largest container with water, and start the whole process moving by filling one of the smaller containers with water and pouring from that container into another. Then, fill another container and pour into another. Continue filling various containers one at a time. There is nothing complex happening, yet children can spend hours, completely absorbed, pouring water from one container to another. Children have a fascination with water, and they just love to play with it and in it.

To avoid having to clean up after all this, go to a local thrift store and buy a lot of used containers just for this purpose, or save plastic containers that you purchase food in. Put them all in a big bucket and never use them for anything else. That way, when the play is over, all you have to do is put the containers in the bucket, store it away somewhere, and put your child in the tub to clean up and finish the experience.

The Art of Storytelling

In the Oak Meadow approach to learning, storytelling has great significance. Some parents and teachers might view storytelling as something that may help the child to feel more secure or bring a few moments of happiness, but do not see stories as a powerful educational tool. At Oak Meadow, we believe that storytelling is one of the most important skills that a teacher can develop. What is it about storytelling that is so important?

Storytelling is something that children of all ages love, and it can lead to some wonderful experiences together for both children and adults. Through storytelling, parents and teachers can create a magical space, where children and adults can experience deeper realities and communicate in ways they rarely do otherwise.

Children will love almost any story that is told to them, simply because the very act of having someone tell you a story gives you a feeling of security and contentment that is rarely found in any other experience. This is because a story creates a "safe space," psychologically and emotionally. While the story is going on, the child enters into a state of timelessness, created by the knowledge that, while this story is happening, nothing else is going on. In addition, if the adult who is telling the story is someone the child knows and loves, the child enters into a state of trust, in which they become completely receptive to the experience that is occurring. These two elements of trust and timelessness are qualities that are conducive to a deeper experience, and when you add to that the uplifting experience provided by a story that has genuine humor or deeper meaning, the total experience is quite extraordinary, both for the child and the adult telling the story.

The basic skill of a storyteller is the ability to draw others into the experience of what is being told. In telling stories to younger children, we often read from a book or tell the story from memory, and sometimes we even create stories that have never been told before. Whatever the source of the story may be, it is usually not based on concrete physical facts, but is drawn from myths, legends, or archetypal themes. However, this lack of physical basis in no way detracts from the importance of the story, for the greatest truths known to humanity are often hidden in such stories, and so they are far more important and more real, especially to young children, than the stories based on hard facts or mundane reality.

Older children also enjoy stories immensely, and their need to experience stories is as deep as it is for younger children. With adolescents, the teacher can utilize the benefits of storytelling most effectively by telling stories that use the basic facts of the subject as guidelines, and imbuing them with life. In this way, the facts virtually "come alive" through the being of the storyteller, and children begin to experience the life of the subject, not just the form. As such, a creative teacher will use the facts of a situation as background scenery in a fascinating story, and draw the children into a real experience of the subject that will have meaning to them.

Most people have read stories aloud from a book, which is an excellent place to start. You can also develop your storytelling skills by creating original stories, which gives you yet another powerful tool to help children transform themselves.

Choosing Stories

In choosing stories for children, it is helpful to consider the child's age and the purpose of the story. There are many wonderful stories to be told, but a thrilling story for a twelve-year-old is usually too complex for a seven-year-old to follow and enjoy. Stories for younger children usually have a very simple plot, uncomplicated characters, and move along rather quickly. As the age of the child increases, the plots generally become more complex, the characters display more subtleties, and more attention is given to detail to bring a greater depth and richness to the overall story.

When we tell stories from memory, we have more freedom to adjust the story than when we read it aloud from a book. So, when telling a story from memory, if the story is a little too complex for a younger child to understand, it can often be adapted by leaving out some of the details. Conversely, a very simple story can be made more enjoyable for older children by adding details to the plot and subtleties to the characters.

When choosing a story, you'll want to consider the purpose of the story. We tell stories for varying reasons: to help lighten a melancholy mood, to share a laugh together, to convey a deep truth, to learn about a particular time period or explore a particular theme, or maybe just to help a scattered child become focused. Whatever the purpose may be, by considering beforehand the elements in the story, you will be better able to choose one that meets the needs of the situation.

Above all, remember and respect your child's needs and sensibilities. It is very important, in choosing a story, to respect this safe space that has been created, and not to violate the receptive, trusting attitude of the child by choosing or creating a story that will leave the child with unresolved or upsetting feelings. This doesn't mean that we can't choose or create stories that contain elements of discord or conflict because these certainly are part of the human condition, and any story would be quite boring without them. However, we have to make sure that these elements are resolved in some way before the story is finished. This way, the child comes out of the story feeling whole and restored. It is especially important for young children to see reflected in their literature an abiding sense that good conquers evil and love is stronger than hate. These underlying themes will feed your child's perception that the world is a good place to live, and nurture a desire to create good in the world.

Telling the Story

Once you have decided which story to tell, there are several elements that will help you create the magic of the story, which is what gives the story its potency and its transforming capabilities.

- First, be fully present. Try to put aside the worries and distractions of the day while you are experiencing the story with your child. This is important for both of you, so that you can have your own moment of escape with your child. Children can sense when your mind is elsewhere and will react with less interest. The main thing about a story that really attracts children is the sense of power that builds as a story is being read or told. Being fully present helps you convey and maintain this literary tension.

- Second, use your voice expressively. Change the tone of your voice as the story seems to call for it, reflecting the differences in the characters and the qualities they represent. A monotone delivery can make even the best story seem dull. Of course, you don't have to adopt a completely different voice for each character! Just try to vary your tone of voice, and use inflection to indicate the different lines that are being spoken. Express the character's surprise, sadness, anger, confusion, teasing, etc. This makes the story characters feel more real and more relevant. You might think of it as performing the story as a radio or movie voice-over actor might do. Changing the tone of your voice in this way brings a greater range of feeling to the overall story, which helps to strengthen the potency of the mood that is created.

- Third, vary the pace of the story. Even if we change our tone of voice, the story can become stagnant unless we vary the pace. Use the events of the story as a guide to the pace, slowing down during the more dramatic, important times, speeding up to heighten the sense of excitement during those periods of the story, and using a more steady pace during the other parts. In this way, the story begins to come alive with life and action. These changes in pace also help children keep their awareness focused on the story because a change of pace draws attention to what is occurring at that moment, and keeps the listener connected with the movement of the story.

- Fourth, support your voice. This means you will consciously project yourself through your voice, so that the voice becomes a vehicle for what you want to accomplish through the story you are telling. This doesn't mean you have to speak loudly, like an actor in a theater, but that the quality of your voice comes across as strong and well-supported. In order to do this, you must first become aware of the location of your voice, that is, the place in which you can feel your voice resonating or vibrating in your body. This can be anywhere from the top of your head to your diaphragm. Unless you have done a lot of public speaking or singing, you will probably find your voice coming from somewhere in your head, often from the sinus cavities, which gives the voice a "nasal" quality. Generally, our voices do not tend to naturally arise from a great depth within us; we must learn how to develop our voices to do this with intention. By bringing your voice more deeply into your body, it can bring a greater fullness to your spoken words.

Developing Your Voice

The voice is a powerful tool. When we speak from a place of strength, our voices reflect this, and those around us are influenced by what we say, whether we are telling stories or asking a simple question. When the voice is used consciously, it can literally transform children. Many parents can attest to this as a "no-nonsense" voice gets immediate results!

However, in order to do this, the voice must be integrated in the body. A voice that emanates from the head is not fully integrated in the body, and thus has no power. When a voice arises more deeply from within the body—from the throat, the chest, or the diaphragm—it becomes magnetic, charismatic. If you want to become a more effective storyteller, try becoming aware of the location of your voice and integrate it more fully into your body.

Stage actors are trained to bring the voice further into the body by projecting it from the diaphragm (the muscle just below the lungs). With practice, the voice can actually be felt physically resonating and vibrating in that region.

Try this experiment in supporting your voice with the diaphragm. Find a place to practice this where you are comfortable and not around others who might be bothered by your voice fluctuations. It also helps if you have something to say that sounds impressive, something that you could imagine saying to a huge crowd of people. For starters, try saying Abraham Lincoln's Gettysburg address, the one that starts, "Four score and seven years ago, our forefathers brought forth on this continent a nation conceived in liberty, and dedicated to the proposition that all men are created equal." When you speak these words, place your hand on your diaphragm, and feel it activating as you draw the air deeper into your lungs and use it to support your energetic speaking. Keep trying to pull your voice deeper from your body, using your internal structures to support and shape the sound.

This is a good exercise for integrating the voice deeper into the body, but we don't need to speak from the diaphragm in everyday life. If you were telling a story in a large hall to a thousand children, you would probably want to speak from the diaphragm to enable everyone to hear you clearly, and to feel the full power of your words. If you are telling a story to one child, sitting in a bedroom at night, speaking at this level would seem ridiculous. For most storytelling you will be doing, you will want your voice to come from your throat or from the region of the chest. By working on your own with simple speaking exercises, you will begin to gain control of where your voice is centered in your body, and to use this to your advantage.

In addition to an integrated, fully supported voice, pay attention to the tonal quality of your voice, and refine it so that it is strong and clear. Children respond instinctively to a person's voice, and will often completely disregard what someone says if the voice conveys uncertainty and lack of power. At the same time, they will readily respond to another person asking the very same thing because that person's voice has a strength and clarity to it. The primary factor is awareness. If you are aware of your voice and pay close attention to what you convey through your words, you can develop an authentic and engaging voice.

Likewise, your tone of voice should be in alignment with what you are saying and your intentions. A good example of this is when a parent says, "Time to go to bed," but says it in a tone of voice that is questioning: "What do you think? Time to go to bed?" The child who isn't interested in going to bed will be happy to answer, "No!" But if you fully intend for it to be bedtime and your voice conveys that tone, there is no question about it: bedtime it is!

How does this apply to effective storytelling? It is important to use your tone of voice in a way that enhances the story. You don't want to develop a phony voice when storytelling, for that would not be beneficial for you (and your children would laugh at you anyway). What is needed is a voice that is comfortable, natural, but resonant. That type of voice has power and presence, and can fully convey the nuances of a story in a way that affects transformations in children.

It may take a while to consciously integrate your voice more fully into your body and then to speak consciously from that place. However, the more you are able to do this—in your teaching, parenting, conversations, and storytelling—the more potency your words will begin to have.

Creating Stories

After you have developed your ability to read stories aloud and tell them from memory, it's time to begin creating your own stories, for this is the full flowering of the storyteller's art. This doesn't mean writing stories for publication, but rather learning how to create stories to be told from memory at a later time, or to create stories spontaneously, while you are actually with children in the midst of the learning process. Creating your own stories is not nearly as difficult as it may seem at first, and the best way to improve in your ability to do this is simply to do it.

Although there are many wonderful stories already published in story books, there are two reasons that the ability to create new stories is important:

- One of the most effective ways to help a child with a problem is by telling a story that has particular relevance for that particular child in that particular situation. In such situations, you may be able to remember a story that will fit the needs of the exact situation, but that is not always possible. In that case, the only other solution is to create it yourself. Creating stories spontaneously with children is a very effective way of creating a bond of love and respect between you. Creating stories spontaneously is also one of the most effective ways to help a child develop the capacity of creative imagination. By playing a game in which you both create a story together (you tell one part, then your child tells the next part, etc.), the child learns how to draw upon their creative imagination in each moment. This can have widespread benefits throughout life, for this is one of the most practical abilities one can have in a world that daily presents us with new challenges.

- The ability to imagine creatively, to move beyond events and situations that exist in front of us and to consider different approaches, is an essential part of human development. Without this ability, many people live "on automatic," never really questioning what they are doing and why they are doing it, but just reacting to whatever the day brings. When we live our lives in this way, we never are able to catch a glimpse of the tremendous possibilities that lie within us because we only are responding to the events in our lives. By unfolding our ability to imagine new possibilities, however, we can begin to manifest those possibilities. The quality of our lives is connected with our ability to draw forth the creative forces within us and imagine things that are not immediately apparent. Creative storytelling helps us develop this capacity.

The act of creating a story spontaneously requires you to connect with your own creative power and express that on a moment-to-moment basis. With this in mind, let's begin considering how to create stories.

All stories have three main elements, and the interaction of these elements create the story. These elements are familiar because they are part of every story and are the same elements we live every day: setting, characters, and plot.

Setting

The story has to happen somewhere and sometime. It can be in a castle far away a long time ago, in a small town during the Depression, in a big city after World War II, in a foreign country today, or on another planet 2,000 years from now. This establishes the time/space framework of the story, and (like all time/space frameworks) places some limitations on what can happen. You'll want to give some consideration to your setting because it has an effect on the story. Of course, you don't have to stay in that place for the whole story if you don't want, but that's where it begins, and if and when you take the story to another setting, you'll have to consider how you're going to do that, and what effect that setting will have on the plot. In most cases, you'll want the setting to "serve" the plot—that is, there has to be a good reason to set the story when and where you do. The reason can be that your character needs to be there (say, a sheepherder) or the plot (say, a story of a rescue in the mountains) needs to happen there.

Characters

Characters are those who populate your story. They don't need to be human, but often are as we find it very easy to relate to other humans. We also find it easy to relate to animals, which is why animal stories are so popular with children. Consider your characters carefully because, again, they must serve the story. Whether you have a weak boy or a strong old woman, your characters have to make sense in terms of what is happening in the story. The primary characters are the main focal point for the story, and secondary characters are those that serve a particular purpose: the bus driver, king, best friend, etc. In stories that are to be told to children, it is best to keep the characters clear and straightforward, rather than full of complex and subtle motives.

Plot

The plot is what the story is about. It is what the characters do within the context of the setting. The plot can be anything you want it to be, and it can end however you want it to end, but do remember the consideration mentioned earlier: respect the safe space that is created by the story. There are many kinds of plots, and in stories intended for adults the plots can often be very convoluted and complex.

Generally, however, for stories that are going to be told to children, the plot (as with the characters) should be simple and direct. For instance, a very basic plot might be this: A child loses a beloved pet and convinces the entire town to help her search for it (of course, they find it in the end, alive and well!). Here's another one: Two brothers are fighting about how to divide up the family farm after their parents die, but when a neighboring farmer tries to cheat them out of their land, the two brothers band together to keep the farm intact.

Most plots in children's stories unfold in three basic stages:

The Opening: This sets the stage for what is to follow. The characters are introduced, the setting is described, and the initial direction of the story begins to unfold. This is when the main story problem is introduced.

The Conflict: The main character begins to encounter obstacles in the situation that was established in the opening. Symbolically, this is where the darkness begins to appear. The majority of the story deals with this problem. A character can experience any kind of conflict. For example, it may be a struggle with another character or group of characters, with some obstacle of nature, or a struggle within themselves.

The Resolution: The main character overcomes the obstacles and achieves the victory. It is quite common in adult stories for the main character to not overcome the obstacles, and the story is resolved by that character's acceptance of the inevitability of their situation. Although this may possibly have benefit for adults, such an ending is generally not appropriate for children. For children's stories, you want a resolution that is clear and direct, and leaves readers or listeners with a satisfying feeling of completion. You want your main character to accomplish what they set out to do.

Creating a Story to Be Told Later

There are many ways to begin a story, but all of them usually involve starting with one element, and having the rest of the story grow from that. The element that you begin with may be tied in with the purpose of the story, or it may just be a picture that you see in your imagination. Whatever it is, you begin to play with that image, and see what develops.

For example, suppose that the purpose of the story is to create an image that can be used to teach the sound and shape of the letter M. When we look at the letter M, we immediately think of a mountain. We play with this image, widening our scope, and asking questions that take us deeper into the story. Are the mountains green and rolling, or high and rocky? Perhaps we see high, rocky mountains. What feeling do they convey? Perhaps they seem harsh and impenetrable. If so, what might be on the other side? A lush valley? And what is in the valley? An image of a little cottage comes to mind, with smoke rising from the chimney. We look into the windows of the cottage, and what do we see? An old man? A young girl? A happy family? Perhaps we see an old man and a young girl. The girl is sad. Why is she sad? Is she lonely or sick? She is lonely, perhaps. Why is she lonely? Maybe she misses her mother. Where is her mother? Over the mountains, in the forest? Why? Maybe the mother couldn't support her daughter, and she had to send the daughter to live with her grandfather, who is old and sick. Perhaps the girl must take care of her grandfather and take care of the farm work too. One day the grandfather dies, and the young girl finds herself alone. She decides to return to her mother, but to do so, she must earn money to help her mother, and then must cross the high rocky mountains.

In this way, from the initial image, we have created the opening for the story. The main character, the setting, and the general plot have been established. To complete this opening stage, we need to describe the setting more fully, tell more about the characters, and begin to develop the details of the plot.

Next we move into the conflict part of the story. Obviously, if the young girl has to earn money and travel across the mountains, she will encounter many obstacles. You don't have to decide in advance what these obstacles will be. Just set the girl on her journey, and follow the images that arise as she progresses, in the same way that the opening was developed. Perhaps the girl becomes depressed, and almost gives up several times, but something happens that gives her new hope. Perhaps she finds a mentor along the way, or a magical coin to help her. As you fill in the details, you move through the conflict stage.

Now, you reach the story's resolution. The girl overcomes the last (and biggest) obstacle, and accomplishes her goal. She is reunited with her mother, she brings money, gold, jewels, a magic hen, or whatever to help support the household, and they live happily ever after.

You have completed your story. Now you can review it and make any changes you want. At this point, you may want to write it down, or you may keep it in your head. Once you have gone over your story and are satisfied with it, you are ready to tell it to the children.

Creating a Story Spontaneously

Once you have practiced a few times with creating stories to be told later, you can begin to create stories spontaneously, and to tell them to an audience as you create them. At first, this may seem to be an almost impossible task. However, after you have done it a few times, you will find that it isn't nearly as difficult as it seems. In some ways, it is easier and more enjoyable than any other form of storytelling because it brings a sharpness to your perceptions and a spontaneity to your actions that is truly exhilarating.

The key to successfully creating stories spontaneously lies in one essential element: the ability to act on your perceptions. In almost every respect, the process of creating a story spontaneously is exactly the same as the process of creating a story to be told later. However, spontaneous storytelling gets its unique character from the fact that you must speak the images that arise within you in the moment they arise, based on what you are picking up from the environment, from your listeners, and from your own inner impulses. This requires a higher degree of awareness since you don't have the opportunity to carefully consider your choices, but in this respect, it is very similar to our experiences in life. Life itself is like one big improvisation because we can never know exactly what will happen or plan for every contingency in advance.

When you begin to tell a story spontaneously, you will consider your audience and the purpose of the story. If there is a particular image that needs to be part of the story, then start with that. Sometimes the children will want a very specific kind of story: "Tell us a story about a rabbit who learned to fly!" Other times, you will begin with your own image. In any event, you will probably need to take a few seconds to clear your mind and to figure out where to start, that is, the nature of the setting, the characters, and the general plot. Children can be remarkably patient while you prepare to tell the story— it's as though the delicious feeling of anticipation holds them in suspense.

Once you have an image to begin with, start describing it, and then follow that along and narrate the progress of the character as the story unfolds. That's really all there is to it!

Beyond that, there are just two important points to remember. First, don't stop to think. If you allow yourself to stop and consider what might be the best action to take, or what color the lion is, or whether the princess meets a witch or a dragon, you will lose the flow of the process. If a purple and green lion occurs to you, then say it. If you see a witch and a dragon, then include both of them. Whatever happens, just keep moving. The object is not to think about what the character will do, but just to be aware and speak the images that arise in your imagination as you proceed.

The second tip is don't worry about whether or not you are doing a good job. You have nothing to be anxious about in this process. It is meant to be an enjoyable experience for you and your children. If you do lose your story thread in the middle, just take a deep breath and start moving again. Your children will not be judging you—they just want to know what happens next!

When creating any kind of story, try to remember this: there are no rules. If you are creating the story, you can create it however you want, and nobody can say you did it wrong. It just isn't possible to create a story wrong. Children are especially accepting when it comes to original stories. They may complain about a story that is printed in a book and that someone bought in a store because they have certain expectations for books. When they know that you made a story up yourself, however, they usually won't be critical of it as long as you sincerely gave it your best effort. So when you begin creating a story, relax, and enjoy the process.

Now that we have looked at some of the elements involved in creating and telling stories, let's consider two specific kinds of stories: the nature story and the archetypal story.

Nature Stories

Telling nature stories is an important part of the Oak Meadow curriculum in the early grades. Nature stories are based on actual events that occur in nature. They can focus on specific subjects like geology, physics, or botany, but for children in the early grades, these story often focus on simple cycles in plant and animal life. Telling nature stories requires specific knowledge, so depending on the topic and the purpose of the story, you may want to do research before creating a nature story.

Learning to tell nature stories for young children requires a sense of reverence for the mysteries of nature, and a desire to share that sense of reverence with children. Sharing the beauty and mystery of the natural world in story form is deeply satisfying and can help your child develop a strong sense of Earth stewardship.

Walk outside and look at the deep blue of the sky. If it is raining, feel the water falling on your face and hands, bringing new life to the thirsty flowers beneath your feet. Walk over to the nearest tree and look closely at a leaf, following the subtlety of the colors and imagining the long journey of water from the roots to the leaf. Nature stories can be made from simple elements such as these. The plot doesn't have to be complicated because these basic processes of nature are the focus of the story. In fact, if the plot is complex, it will detract from the sense of wonder that should pervade the story.

In general, nature stories can be created from almost any aspect of the world of nature, and the simpler the story, the better. Possibilities for stories include:

- The beginning and end of a rainstorm
- The cycle of growth of a seed
- The building of a bird's nest
- The blossoming of a flower
- The yearly cycle of a tree

As you can see, the suggestions given all involve processes of nature. This is because it is easier to create a story around something that has movement and growth than around something that is static. Focus on the rhythms and cycles of nature, and on the interconnectedness of nature and all living things. You don't have to create imaginary characters or clever dialogue; just relate what happens in a way that has meaning. For example, if you were to tell a story about the cycle of growth of a seed it might sound something like this:

> Let me tell you about the most amazing thing in the world. Do you know what happens to an apple when it falls off a tree? It lies on the ground and the sun shines on it and the rain falls on it and it begins to rot. You know of course what someone means when they say something is rotten. It means that it is dying; the life that was in it that made it good to eat is going out of it. Well, that is what happens to the apple: it dies. And slowly all of the part that is good to eat falls away back into the earth or is eaten by worms.

> But one very important part is left. That is called the seed. The seed is the part in the very center of the apple—a little, tiny, hard thing that is very magical. The reason it is so magical is this: from that tiny little seed can grow a whole apple tree filled with hundreds of apples year after year. Just from that one tiny seed!

> But before that can happen, something special has to take place. The seed has to lie on the ground and be heated by the sun and soaked by the rain until finally the earth covers it completely so that you can't even see it anymore. By that time, it is usually winter outside. The air is cold, the snow may be falling, but the seed is in the earth, protected by the earth from all that goes on above.

And in that darkness, when all seems to be lost, when the seed is buried in the earth, the magical thing starts happening. Somewhere from within that seed, life begins to move. And very slowly the seed begins to swell and grow. Then the seed splits open and a tiny little sprout begins to rise up toward the light above. It struggles hard, day after day, pushing earth out of the way and reaching for the light.

Then, one day, it breaks through the soil and feels the warmth of the sun and the cool breezes blowing. Now it is spring. Days go by and the little sprout grows bigger and bigger in the sun and rain. After years and years of growing, the little sprout that was once just a tiny seed is now a big apple tree, with many, many juicy apples hanging from its branches.

Of course, that same story could be told in countless ways, but the essence will always be the same.

In telling nature stories, try to tell it in an archetypal form, using symbols of light and darkness, or birth and death, instead of scientific concepts and terms, such as photosynthesis. There is time enough for that in the later years. By sharing your reverence for the mysteries of nature, you will be helping children to slowly grow in understanding of these processes and deepen love for the beauty of life.

Archetypal Stories

The fundamental idea of archetypes arises from the writings of Plato and has influenced human beings ever since. Essentially, the basic concept is that all physical forms and activities are reflections of deeper realities (which Plato called *archetypes*), much the same as the image that we see in a mirror is not the reality itself, but a reflection of that reality. By observing the events that occur in the world through the lens of archetypes, we can begin to understand and experience the deeper realities that form the underlying framework.

Archetypal stories are appropriate for children and adults of all ages, although usually they are most popular with children ages 6 to 12. Archetypal stories have always been very popular among children, as evidenced by the rich heritage of fairy tales within the literature of almost every culture. Modern classics, such as *The Wonderful Wizard of Oz* and The Chronicles of Narnia series, are archetypal stories—their enduring popularity speaks to the inner power of these stories.

Filmmakers also create films based on stories that are deeply archetypal in nature. These types of stories and movies deal with the battle between light and dark, and express this battle in various ways, but all use forms that are symbolic of inner experiences. Chances are that when you read a story that is especially meaningful to you, it has archetypal elements that are speaking to the shared elements of the human experience.

Of course, telling a story that does not use archetypes does not automatically ensure that the story will be shallow and meaningless. However, your stories are likely to be more powerful, meaningful, and memorable if you use archetypes. This is the secret of most fairy tales. They incorporate archetypal symbols and are able to lift us out of our dreary day-to-day realities and give us a sense of the greatness within us all. These stories use clear images of good and evil and then take us through a struggle against overwhelming forces. We feel certain that all is lost, but our courage and persistence allow us to triumph in the end. In this way, archetypal stories remind us of our deeper nature and of the real importance of the life experience.

Learning how to use archetypes is not as difficult as it may seem at first, because we are all players in the same drama. Archetypes speak to the universal human drama. So learning how to use archetypes in storytelling is not so much a matter of learning something new as it is becoming aware of that which we already know. Archetypal stories are not always of the castle/prince/dragon variety, of course. It's the symbolism of the story that makes it archetypal and not the particular forms involved.

Here are some classic archetypal images that are found in stories around the world:

- The hero/warrior
- The villain
- The mother or father figure
- The innocent child
- The trickster or joker

Here are some classic archetypal story themes:

- The hero's journey
- The loss of innocence (or initiation into adulthood)
- Good versus evil
- Eternal love
- The quest for knowledge

The best way to begin an archetypal story is by glimpsing a central image and then working (or play-ing) with it. This central image can be a battle between archetypal elements, such as the head and the heart (intellect versus passion/compassion), or this image may simply be a character that expresses a certain quality, such as perseverance or greed. Whatever this initial image may be, the rest of the story can grow from it as you access your creative mind and give outer forms to the fundamental elements of the human experience.

The Importance of Fairy Tales

One of the central themes of the Oak Meadow early grades curriculum is one of offering children the opportunity to develop their imaginative capacities by introducing subject content through rich story images. Stories (particularly those without pictures) allow children the chance to enhance their innate ability to see and feel characters, landscapes, interactions, gestures, predicaments, and solutions in their mind's eye. Children also connect with these characters and events on an emotional, or heart, level thereby developing their ability to experience alternate perspectives or feel compassion for another's situation.

These capacities are foundational blocks in a child's later ability to understand other times, places, and perspectives, and to use imaginative skills in solving real life and academic problems. For example, the imaginative capacity is necessary when contemplating mathematical equations, when meeting adversity, when learning about historical events and cultures, when considering scientific and natural phenomena, and when expressing oneself through music, art, movement, or conversation. In addition, stories told aloud create a unique connection between listener and storyteller, one that gives the child the feeling of being acknowledged and tended to, an increasingly important event in today's fast-paced world.

In language arts, fairy tales are used to introduce students to the form, name, and sounds of letters of the alphabet by painting for them colorful, diverse, and lively internal images. Since the letters of the alphabet are abstract in nature, stories are told to children as a way to support them in connecting with the letters out of their own activity. An example can easily be seen when introducing the sound and shape of the letter M. A story is often told that includes a mountain. As the child hears the story, they begin to see the mountain's peaks, craggy landscape, or running rivers. The next day, the child recalls and describes the story elements, thereby strengthening their memory for story details and sequencing. Then they are guided in some kind of artistic activity based on the image of the mountain, "discovering" the form on the M within the peaks. Now, the letter M has meaning and context for the child, not only due to the strong images from the story, but also due to recalling story details and exercising will through artistic expression. This is a lovely example of the experience of working with **head** (recalling the story), **heart** (connecting with the story content imaginatively), and **hands** (expressing connection through artistic activity.)

Fairy tales were chosen to introduce young children to letters and sounds, not only due to their very rich images, but also as a way to meet children in their unique developmental stage. Though fairy tales differ with respect to characters and events, they all have in common the polarity of good versus bad. To children in kindergarten and first grade, this polarity is understood as an expression of the inner experience as they mature out of early childhood—the pull of the polarities within them. This school-aged child is beginning to know and understand rules and behavioral expectations of the family and the wider society, yet they have yet to develop firm impulse control, contextual thinking, and the ability to think reflectively. The good versus bad polarity mirrors the child's inner experience of knowing what might be expected of them, and the pull toward the opposite (doing what they want rather than what should be done). A child may hear from the family that it's "good" to speak and act calmly, respectfully, and kindly, yet they sometimes feel and act angry, jealous, greedy, and naughty. Thus the fairy tale speaks directly to the child as it acknowledges the range of human impulses and experiences.

Though adults might read the fairy tale and identify with characters quite literally, children experience the characters not as individual people, but as aspects of themselves, in an unconscious connection with the archetypal image. Children hear about the evil stepmother, and their own feelings of sometimes acting selfishly are acknowledged. They hear about the prince and princess going through travails in order to marry or claim their birthright, and children are validated and affirmed in their own work at combining their feminine and masculine traits or standing up for themselves and being true to their own inner nature. When children hear about the powerful dragon that destroys a village only to be tamed by the brave knight, they are encouraged by the possibility of taming their own fears by connecting with their own bravery and courage. When they hear about a character who is lost in the dark only to be rescued by a creature of the forest, children are comforted by the idea that times of darkness are followed by times of hope.

In essence, the characters of the fairy tale are uniquely well-suited to meet children because children innately think in archetypes rather than stereotypes. The fairy tale speaks strongly to young children because good always prevails over bad, and this is what children need to hear as they step out into the world. Perhaps most poignantly for the child, when told a fairy tale by their loved ones, it tells the child that they understand and validate this inner struggle. If the parent is able to express the evil elements in the story without making judgments, then it tells the child that their feelings and struggles are worthy. In this way, the adult offers valuable support and compassion for the child's journey toward maturity.

It is important for parents and teachers to keep in mind that the young child does not naturally think in such literal terms as adults tend to do. When preparing to read or tell a fairy tale to your child, read through the fairy tale first before telling it so that you can familiarize yourself with the images. Reading the story by yourself a day ahead gives you time to reflect on and come to terms with any story elements that may have hit a nerve.

When you can identify the elements you struggle with, and remind yourself of the different nature of a child's thinking compared to yours, the fairy tale can be offered to the child freely and without adult interpretation. This allows the child to take from the story what is meaningful and necessary to them at that time.

After telling the fairy tale, it's best to refrain from guiding the child in analytical questioning. Literary analysis will come in later years, but for now, the intention of the story recall is simply to support the child in remembering actual events and the sequence in which they happened. The focus of the recall should be centered on guiding the child in remembering what and when things happened, rather than asking why the child thinks something happened as it did or asking the child to give an opinion on the story. Let the fairy tale's powerful archetypal images simply feed the child's rich imagination and inner experiences.

Art Instruction

Artistic expression is a very important part of the Oak Meadow curriculum because we believe it is an important element of the human experience. The primary media used throughout the curriculum are beeswax crayons, watercolor paints, modeling beeswax, and clay. Crayon drawing is used extensively as children create their own main lesson books. Watercolor painting offers a unique expression of flowing color and form, and it helps to develop an understanding of the subjective value of colors. Modeling with beeswax and clay gives children the opportunity to create three-dimensional forms with their hands, pairing artistry and imagination with practicality.

Any activity can be approached in a considered, focused manner (consciously) or haphazardly (unconsciously). Art is no exception. If an artistic activity is approached consciously, it can open opportunities for the expression of the rich inner world within the individual.

In many educational situations, children are not given much (if any!) guidance in the early stages of artistic activity. Children are often left on their own to learn to draw, paint, and sculpt, and after they pass through the early years of gleeful, unselfconscious abandon, begin to doubt their artistic abilities within a few short years. It's not uncommon to hear a child in third or fourth grade say, "I can't draw," a sentiment echoed wholeheartedly by the majority of adults.

However, once these children (or adults) set aside their doubts and approach artistic activities with open and willing head, heart, and hands, most discover that they can learn to draw and benefit from creating art as much as any accomplished artist. By consciously helping your child learn to draw, paint, and sculpt in the early years, you are opening doors to a world of creative opportunities.

Crayon Drawing

As imitation is the child's primary means of learning in the early grades, the best way you can teach your child to draw is to participate fully in drawing. If you have a chalkboard (and good quality chalk in a wide selection of colors) or your own main lesson book, you can demonstrate drawing technique for your child, who will initially copy your work. This lets your child learn in a natural, organic way, by copying what you do, rather than approaching it from an intellectual viewpoint of angles, lines, colors, shading, etc. Formal art instruction will come in fourth grade, but for now, it is most beneficial for your child to simply imitate your actions.

The illustrations that you will be doing for your child to copy are simple, basic forms. These forms encourage a child's early experiences in artistic expression and can be easily created by any parent willing to try. Sophisticated talent is not necessary, and in many cases can be a detriment as children will not find themselves able to copy a professional level drawing.

In the early stages of development, children tend not to focus on forms as sharply as an adult, but rather see the world more as an interplay of changing colors, shapes, and inner feelings. Thus, the appropriate artistic forms for imitation by a child just learning to draw are not detailed figures or line drawings (or stick figures), but full shapes composed of rich natural colors without intricate details. As the child's objective awareness of the world grows, the shapes will gradually become more detailed, reflecting this change in awareness. But a child shouldn't be pressured into expressing detail too early, for it has the effect of bringing forth the mental faculties too early, which can result in a premature development of the critical nature, causing unhappiness in parent and child alike.

You will note that in the lessons, children are often asked to draw illustrations of a story they have heard and to include specific story details in the story. This should not be confused with a detailed picture. A story detail might be Little Red Riding Hood's red hood or her basket. These story details can be drawn in a very simple form, without the need for artistic details, such as a tie for the hood or a blue checkered napkin in the basket. This type of detail will show up in a child's drawings when they are ready; until then, simply focus on encouraging the inclusion of story details, not artistic detail.

Tips on Teaching a Child to Draw

As you begin to experiment with drawing and with teaching your child to draw, you will find the illustrations in the lessons to be helpful. You are encouraged to copy them, if you'd like, until you feel more confident in your own drawing skills. These illustrations are designed to help children express themselves through the use of rich colors and full figures, drawing "from the inside out," rather than outlining a form and coloring it in.

We highly recommend using beeswax block crayons for drawings, and beeswax stick crayons for writing in the first and second grades, switching to colored pencils for writing in third grade. The block crayons provide a particularly forgiving experience for children learning to draw. They do take some getting used to, however, and we recommend you taking some time to explore how to use the different edges to create shapes or drag the crayon across the page to lay down a large swath of color for, say, the sky or ground.

Block crayons make it easy to form shapes from the inside out, and allow a child to use softer, more muted lines rather than the bold lines often made by stick crayons. Coloring an oval shape that becomes a person's body, with a smaller oval on top for the head, and long thin ovals for limbs, all colored using the wide strokes of a block crayon, helps children see and feel the human form emerge organically. The shapes feel fully formed when drawing in this manner, as though they have substance and are not just a flat drawing on a page.

As a practical guide to understanding the means of creating full, rich drawings, we offer the following suggestions:

1. **Model and encourage your child to draw shapes from the inside out, instead of outlining.** If a child has spent many years outlining shapes and coloring them in (or using coloring books with bold outlined shapes), it may be challenging to help your child learn a new technique, but with a little persistence and patience, you will both be happier with the results. An outline creates a rigid line, which is immovable, so if the line isn't "right" when it is first drawn, it cannot be adjusted to conform to the image the child is trying to create. This can be a source of great frustration to a child learning to draw.

   Generally, not even an accomplished artist would create an image by first outlining with a bold line. An artist generally creates images using a sequence of lightly drawn lines, drawing the general shape of the form over and over, until the lines gradually merge and darken as the intended image becomes more accurate.

   If you wish to draw a tree, therefore, don't start by doing this:

   Instead, develop the tree as a movement of color rising from the ground, just as a tree would naturally grow.

First, the earth

Next, the root

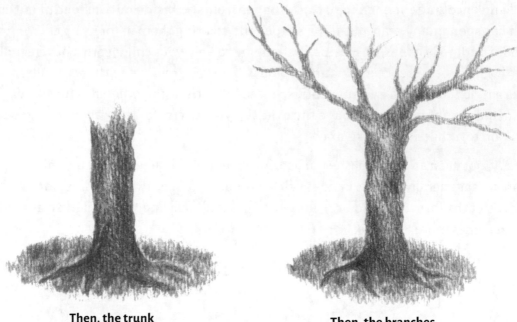

Then, the trunk

Then, the branches

Finally, the leaves

In this way a child is able to adjust the image as it develops, instead of being bound by the first line drawn. The result feels much more organic and authentic.

2. **"Feel your way along." Encourage your child with these words as they draw.** In our example of the tree, this would mean imagining that you are standing in front of the tree and feeling each part of the tree—the roots coming out of the ground, the trunk rising up, the limbs branching off,

etc. As you feel your way in imagination, you move the crayon along the paper, "feeling your way along" with the edge of the crayon. Not only does this often produce a more accurate drawing, but more important, it allows a fuller, richer artistic experience by connecting the inner image with the outer representation.

3. **Show your child how to fill the entire page with color.** Blue sky above should reach all the way to the edges of the page and to the green grass below. If the picture is of the inside of a house, the walls should be colored in, perhaps with something on the walls. Create a feeling of reality about the picture, and an expansive sense of space.

4. **Spend some time practicing on your own before asking your child to do a particular drawing.** This will help give you the confidence to guide your child's work with firm purpose and presence. Remember, your child is not expecting you to be another Rembrandt; focusing your own intention and willingness on learning to draw will help your child to do the same.

In the beginning, it will help your child to have you draw an illustration that they can copy. After a month or so, however, you can begin to encourage them to try drawing now and then without copying from anything. This will help keep your child from believing that they must always copy another drawing. However, remember that imitation is a child's lifeblood in the early years; it is the child's nature. Therefore, you can support your child by creating an imaginary picture through the story that you tell, and make the images strong and clear, so the child has something definite to imitate in drawing. In this way, your child can learn how to give outer form to the images that arise within the imagination.

Don't expect a child to sit down and just create a picture without first having a vivid image planted in the imagination. Most children will need assistance with this before they learn to create vivid, detailed images from their own resources.

Drawing Forth Your Own Inner Artist

As you begin to work with art in your teaching, it may be helpful to reflect on your own artistic process. This can help you present a clear presence to your child, rather than worrying about your own drawings. If you worry that your drawing doesn't look "right," your child is likely to pick up on this and begin worrying about their own drawings.

In the first few weeks of learning to draw, take some time to consider your experience:

1. Were you able to move your crayon on the paper, letting the form arise in an organic way, or did you feel compelled to outline the form first and fill it in? If now you are able to let go of the outline and draw from the inside out, how do you feel about your picture? Does the inner experience of creating art change when you fill in fuller forms rather than outlining?

2. Do you find yourself judging your drawings against the standard of how they are "supposed to look"? What would you say to your child if they crumpled up a drawing, crying that it didn't look like it was supposed to? You would probably find it very easy to say something encouraging

and nonjudgmental about your child's art. Can you be encouraging and nonjudgmental with yourself?

3. Do you feel a need to hurry through your picture or are you comfortable taking a half hour or more to complete a picture? Do you feel yourself becoming calmer as you sink into the process? How does your experience change when you are rushed as opposed to taking the time to consider color choices, running the crayon over and over the form to get the shape that feels right, and setting aside the tasks of the day and a to-do list to just breathe into the experience and enjoy making art? Perhaps you can think of some things that you can do to create an atmosphere of expansive time while your child is drawing, so that it doesn't just feel like another thing that needs to be accomplished so that you can move on.

As you become more aware of your own artistic process, you will be better able to support your child's artistic experience. Together, the two of you can find out the best way for you to open up artistically and get the most out of the creative experience.

Form Drawing

Another artistic activity that you should begin to explore is called form drawing. In addition to developing a greater control of the hand, these exercises foster inner poise and balance, strengthen the imaginative faculties, and unfold an appreciation for order and symmetry. They can become increasingly complex as you continue to develop variations. It is important that the focus always be on quality rather than quantity.

In the Oak Meadow curriculum, we introduce form drawing as part of the math program. Its form and symmetry is an excellent foundation for geometry and spatial awareness. In addition, form drawing leads nicely into cursive handwriting in the third grade. You will find specific directions in the lessons about when and how to use form drawings, but this introduction to form drawing will help you familiarize yourself with the process beforehand.

The exercises are primarily of two types in the early grades. First, the child learns to reproduce a line form drawn by the parent or teacher on a separate paper. Second, the child learns to create a mirror image of a line form drawn by the teacher. In mirror image drawings, the teacher draws one side of a form and the student draws a mirror image of the form. Forms are done in both horizontal and vertical alignment.

Basic Types of Form Drawing

Form drawing exercises are best approached very informally when you have a quiet moment with your child. However, they can also be very helpful if your child has just had a minor emotional upset and needs some attention and something tangible to focus on. The easiest way to begin is simply by sitting down with your child, two pieces of paper, and a pencil. At first, you can introduce your child to the two basic line forms: a straight line and a curved line. You can say that these two kinds of forms are very different, as different as night and day, but everywhere we look, we see these forms. You only have to look around to see that it is true—every form is either straight, curved, or a combination of the two.

As always, evoking a story or image will help your child grasp the concept of form drawings and enter into the experience. You can say that straight and curved lines like to do different things.

For example, if a curved line is running, it might show it like this:

If it is running and hopping, it might show it like this:

But straight lines would rather march than run,

and they don't care to hop, but they will climb walls.

Curved lines can show happiness very easily,

or even sadness.

But when it comes to being cross or irritable, they leave that to the straight line, who can even fight if it has to.

But curved lines would always rather love than fight.

This gives you an idea of the possibilities of simple form drawings (this type is sometimes called a running form, as it runs across the paper, repeating a predictable pattern). As you and your child become familiar with the basic character of straight and curved lines, together you can create many forms to represent shades of feeling or different story scenarios. Always give your child plenty of time to practice each form—it can be harder than it looks, as you will soon see! Once you draw your form, feel free to go over it several times with the crayon, working to smooth out bumpy edges or increase the symmetry of the form. Then, create the form again on a new piece of paper, seeing if you can create a more consistent, accurate form after you have practiced. This is the process your child will go through as well.

Of course, you don't always have to have a certain mood or story attached to the form. As you and your child become more adept at form drawing, it can be fun just to create new forms and take turns reproducing each other's forms.

The second type of form drawing, mirrored form drawings, are beneficial in helping the child integrate the left and right hemispheres of the brain. They also help to develop the imaginative faculties as the form has to be clearly pictured in the mind before it can be copied in reverse. When introducing mirrored form drawings, you might begin by explaining that a line that is perfectly straight and not moving can act as a mirror, just like the mirrors we have in our houses.

Draw a vertical line to be your "mirror," and then draw a simple shape on the left side of the line. Then, pretending that the straight line is a mirror, draw the reflection on the other side.

Start with very simple shapes until your child begins to understand what is meant by a mirror image. When this becomes clear, you can begin to create more challenging shapes. Go very slowly, however, because the benefits from this exercise arise from the focus required to duplicate the form. As with painting one beautiful painting rather than a dozen ones thoughtlessly done, a form drawing takes concentration and should not be rushed.

As you experiment with different shapes, you begin to see that the possibilities of forms are unlimited. In a short time, we can develop more complex forms such as these, all starting with a single vertical line to act as the mirror,

using curved lines,

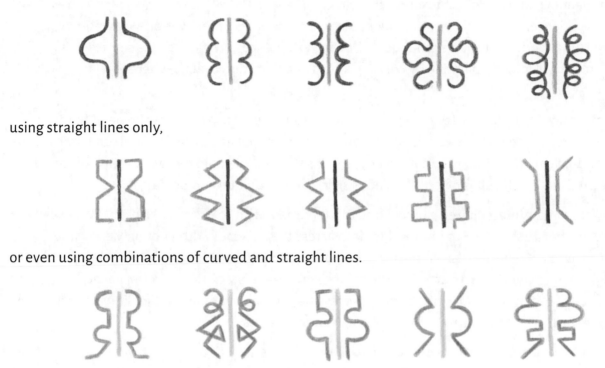

using straight lines only,

or even using combinations of curved and straight lines.

Next, this can be developed in the horizontal realm. In this case the teacher draws the form above, and the child reflects that figure below:

Form drawings can be used to embellish the borders of your child's main lesson books, and they can be used to create decorative cards. Friends and relatives are especially pleased when they receive a hand-made card, rather than one from the store.

As you begin to explore form drawing with your child, be patient with yourself! It takes some time to develop a steady hand and symmetrical, consistent forms. Some people enjoy putting on quiet music to help set a calm mood for form drawing. Others prefer silence so that concentration is encouraged. However you choose to approach your form drawing, just do your best, stay focused, and don't rush. This will encourage your child to do the same.

Watercolor Painting

Watercolor painting is very helpful as a means of expressing feelings that are too elusive and subtle, or too expansive, for crayons. Children are naturally fascinated with the world of color, and this shows clearly in their love of painting. The approach we recommend at Oak Meadow, particularly for early painting experiences, is wet-paper watercolor painting (sometimes called wet-on-wet watercolor painting). This experience provides a uniquely flowing experience, but it does take some getting used to if you are accustomed to painting by creating a bold line that stays exactly where you put it on the page.

When watercolors are used on dry paper, the result is often a very crisp edge, as the paint hardens onto the paper. If, instead, the paper is wet before the paint is applied, it offers opportunity for a wonderful blending of colors. The watercolor paint remains fluid and flexible for the duration of the painting. When it dries, the result is often a luminous swirl of color, unique and beautiful.

With wet-paper painting, children can feel free to experiment with colors and forms without having one stroke of the brush create an immovable slash across the paper. Children not only enjoy the wet-paper approach but they also create more beautiful paintings. In addition, it has the important effect of providing children with an opportunity to develop an appreciation of color, particularly how colors blend to form new colors. The painting process stays in the realm of fluid feeling instead of prematurely focusing the child's attention on the perfection of forms.

To use this painting approach, the following supplies are needed:

- Tubes of watercolor paint in the three primary colors. We recommend watercolors in blue, red, and yellow. These are available in quarter-ounce tubes, which is a convenient size to use. (We suggest using tubes of paint, instead of the cakes of paint found in most paint sets, because the tube paint gives you much more freedom to play with the strength of the colors. It also allows you to mix your own combinations from the primary colors.)

- Watercolor paintbrushes with a broad bristle. We recommend a $\frac{3}{4}$" bristle.

- A sturdy watercolor paper (we recommend 90-pound paper for best results) about 9 x 12 inches in size. You can use 12 x 18 inch paper, but it's more expensive.

These supplies are available at any good art supply store and through Oak Meadow.

Wet-Paper Painting

Using these supplies, the technique that we use for wet-paper painting is as follows:

1. Clear a large flat surface for painting. Put a dab of paint into a dish and then pour a small amount of water (about one ounce) into the dish, and mix the paint into the water thoroughly. If you are using more than one color, put each color in a separate dish to avoid mixing colors. If you are using all three colors you should have three separate dishes. Fill a large container with water—

this is for rinsing the paint off the brushes. Once you have these materials in place, fill a sink with water a few inches deep.

Immerse a sheet of watercolor paper completely under the water and let it soak for a few seconds. Then pick up the paper and let most of the surface water drip back into the sink. Place the wet paper on the flat painting surface, and wipe the excess water off with a damp sponge. The paper should be wet, but not have surface pools of water on it. Experience will help you to find just the right amount of wetness. Glide the sponge over the paper until any air bubbles are smoothed away.

2. Before you start painting, it is helpful to have a clear image of what you would like to paint. Children usually can create an image easily if they've been prepared for it through a story or an imaginative description. For example, maybe you've been telling a story about the sun and the moon, and you want to paint a picture of the sun.

    When you're ready to paint, you might talk about the sun from a "feeling" point of view: how warm it is, how strong it is, how hot it can get on a summer day, how cheerful it can be in the morning. As you speak, your child will naturally be creating images of the sun in their mind. As your child puts brush to paper, those images will be expressed in a natural way. Remember that a child is "seeing" the world not nearly as much through the eyes as through the feelings, so the best way to help your child get a strong image to work with is to recall the feeling of the sun rather than just talk about how it looks.

    It can be helpful for you to paint alongside your child, creating your own images on paper as you talk through the experience. Unlike with crayon drawing, the idea is not for your child to copy your image, but for you to share the creative space with your child and help support a sense of careful thought and presence as you paint. You don't want your child to simply slap paint on the paper. By modeling a clear intention with regard to your own painting, your child is likely to follow suit.

3. When your child has a clear image of what to paint, help decide the best way to approach it. For example, if you want to paint a picture of a yellow sun in a blue sky, you will have to paint the sun first, or else leave a hole in the sky to put the sun in. Otherwise, when you apply yellow paint to a blue sky, you will get a green sun, which probably isn't what you want.

4. Once you see clearly how to begin, dip the brush in one color and start painting. As you are painting, the object is not to try to perfect the form the first time, but to feel your way into the painting, with each dab you make with your brush, much as you felt your way along with the crayon in your drawing. Focus on the experience of how the paint feels as it moves across the paper. Maintain your image of what it is you want to paint, but also watch the direction the painting itself is moving, and try to stay balanced between the two.

    Thus, the entire painting process is one of dabbing the paint in a direction and color that conforms to your image, then pausing to consider how that action has changed the painting; then clarifying and perhaps changing your intention for the painting, then urging it in that direction with another dab from your brush. Continue to pause to consider and feel the next direction as you flow through the painting process. Of course, this explanation is for your understanding and not some-thing your child would need to know or care about. However, if you understand this process, you will communicate that to your child through your painting technique.

5. When the painting is finished, put it aside in a safe place and leave it flat to dry. In a few hours it will be dry enough to move around and hang on the wall. Don't move it around before it is dry or the paint will run and spoil the painting.

Working with Color

The three primary colors are red, yellow, and blue. That is all you need. All the colors of the rainbow can be made from these three. It benefits children greatly to have the freedom to explore these col-ors—and how they blend, on their own—rather than being handed a set of a dozen or more already mixed colors. It is an exciting discovery when a child first experiences how to blend red and yellow to make orange. This leads to more explorations: red and blue make purple, yellow and blue make green, and combinations of these make all the colors in between. If you are painting trees, brown comes from a blending of all three colors.

One word of caution: be sure that the brush is rinsed in the water after each color is used or soon there will only be one color—a dark, muddy mixture of all the colors.

Keep a sponge handy and dab the clean, wet brushes on the sponge before dipping the brush into a new color. This helps prevent your paintings from looking drowned out. Make sure your child cleans the brush after each application of paint, and mix the colors together only on the painting paper, not in the dishes. Each dish of paint should have just one clear color.

If you want to make a secondary color such as green, here's what you do. Put yellow on the brush and apply it where you want it on the paper. Clean your brush in the water, and touch it to the sponge to get rid of any excess water. Put blue on your brush and apply it on top of the yellow on the paper, mix-ing the two colors together until you get a blend you like. By varying the amount of blue or yellow, you can create various shades of green, but you always have to wash your brush in between adding each new color so that your dishes of paint stay clear and true to their original colors.

Before you jump right in with all the colors, have a few sessions where you use only blue, or yellow, or red, and explore the range of shades within each color. This will also give you and your child a chance to experiment with how the watercolor paint blends and moves along the wet paper without having the distraction of multiple colors to explore at the same time. Then have a few sessions where you use two colors—red and yellow, red and blue, blue and yellow—and explore these variations.

The Painting Process

It may help for you to reflect on and process your own feelings after trying wet-paper painting, as this can help you be more aware of your child's experience and needs.

1. Did you enjoy the flexibility that the wet paper provided in this process, or did you feel frustrated because the images seemed out of your control? Next time, try to let go of any preconceived notions about what the painting will look like and just enjoy watching how it evolves.

2. As you applied small strokes to the paper, were you able to see the possibilities and flow easily into the next stroke, or did you feel somewhat uncertain or impatient because there wasn't a definite form to follow? It can help to breathe into the process—actually take a deep breath and breathe out as you move the brush. This can help you focus on the feeling of the paint moving across the page, and become more involved in the changes that happen with each brushstroke.

3. Were you able to engage in painting for an uninterrupted period of time? It is extremely helpful to clear a space in your day so that you know you can stay focused and present without having to worry about phones ringing, something cooking on the stove, or a younger child needing attention.

4. Did you feel able to relax and focus on the creative process? Perhaps your mind felt still, or perhaps you caught yourself drifting off and had to work on disciplining your mind to stay present. Remember, this is a process for you as well as for your child! You are both learning, and benefiting from, the artistic process.

If you found it challenging to relax into the process and to focus on your painting, consider how you can free more of your attention to be present. If you are worried or tense, try physical exercise before your next painting session. Take a walk with your child, or a bike ride, or jump rope, or just go outside for some stretching and a few deep breaths. This can help both of you prepare to settle into the reflective process of painting.

Above all, don't rush the painting process or the artistic experience. Watercolor painting can be an exhausting and messy experience if you rush through 10 to 15 paintings in 15 minutes. On the other hand, it can be a tremendously satisfying and meaningful experience for both you and your child if you focus on doing one painting with patience and sensitivity. So take your time, and explore the world of color and feeling with your child.

Clay Sculpting

Working with clay can be an immensely enjoyable experience. A lack of knowledge about specific techniques doesn't usually keep children and adults alike from diving into the process with both hands and an adventurous spirit! However, a little instruction can help you be better equipped to get the most out of the experience.

Oak Meadow offers a set of clay projects with detailed instructions in *Oak Meadow Crafts for the Early Grades*. The projects are designed especially for children.

Before you begin, you can read the following to your child:

> Clay is found in the earth, formed from the mineral deposits of rocks that have ground down to dust. Over time, mountains are slowly ground into rocks, rocks are slowly ground into sand, and sand is slowly ground into clay.
>
> Early humans discovered what clay would do when it was put into fire. It hardened, making it much more useful and durable. People found that making things with clay was easier and faster than carving wood or stone.
>
> People soon learned to make clay jars for storing grains, water, and vegetables. Pots for eating and cooking were also needed, and clay was used to make them. Special figures were made of clay for ceremonies. Clay, a gift from the earth, became a valuable part of human culture.

This is an excellent time to look around your own house and yard to see what is made of clay.

Tips for Working with Clay

Working with clay is an activity that children find compelling; it can absorb them for hours. However, without a bit of forethought on the parent's part, it can also be a disastrous mess! To help you and your child gain the most appreciation from working with clay, we include the following guidelines.

First, try to find a corner of your house (laundry room, basement, or patio) where a small sturdy table or large board can be set up to use only for working with clay. If it is confined to one area, it greatly lessens the chances of a mess and also makes it more convenient. As clay will sometimes get on walls in the immediate vicinity, cover the walls right around the clay area with some sort of protective covering (newspaper, plastic, wrapping paper, etc.). This can be affixed with thumbtacks and replaced when it becomes too dirty. Put a large flat board (plywood works well) on top of the table.

In addition to a large block of clay (**25** pounds is a good size, and can be found in most craft stores), here are some basic tools to have on hand for working with clay:

- A large container with a tight lid to keep the clay in (very important!)

- A container for water

- An old, large long-sleeved shirt

- Implements for cutting or shaping the clay, such as an old dull table knife, popsicle stick, toothpicks, rolling pin, fork, etc.

- A paintbrush

- Newspaper for drying

- A variety of objects that can be used for making textures, such as a piece of window screen, rough fabric, fresh leaves, shells, etc.

Put these supplies together in a box by the table, or on top of the table if there is room. It helps immensely if everything that is needed is right there so that you don't have to spend your time hunting for everything whenever your child wants to work with the clay.

The most important of these supplies is the large wide-mouth container with a tight lid. If the clay is not exposed to the air, it will last indefinitely. If exposed to air, however, it will dry up quickly and become useless. (If a large container of this sort is not available, a large plastic bag will also work. But if this is used, you must be careful that the bag is not left open, and that the excess is wrapped around the clay to seal out the air.) About 25 pounds of clay should be plenty to meet your needs, if it is not allowed to dry out.

Before you let your child jump into the clay, it is best to sit down and talk over a few of the ground rules so that the clay experience can be enjoyable for both of you. Some of the ground rules that we feel are important are as follows:

1. Put on an old shirt before you start.

2. Don't use the whole supply of clay to work with. Cut off a small piece, return the supply to its container and seal it tightly.

3. Don't soak the clay with water. Use only as much water as you need to smooth the rough areas.

4. Don't throw the clay down on the board. That splatters clay and water all over everything.

5. When you are finished with the piece you are working on, decide whether or not to keep it. If you want to keep it, set the piece aside to dry for about three days. Mold the extra scraps back into the bulk supply and seal the container tightly. If you don't want to keep it, mold all the clay back into the bulk supply and seal the container tightly.

It may be helpful to remind your child that if you save everything you make, the clay will soon be gone. Form the habit of returning 99 percent of the work back into the supply, only saving pieces that are very special. Remember that creations that appear to be full of life often lose a lot of magic when they dry.

Creating Form out of Clay

The last question that needs to be answered is, "What should be made?" If left to their own devices, children will usually try to give form to whatever image is uppermost in their minds. If you just saw a tractor in the field, your child will probably try to make a tractor. If your child doesn't have any particular image in mind, they may just smash the clay around for a while and make a mess. *Oak Meadow Crafts for the Early Grades* includes a wide variety of ideas for projects, and you can also find books in the library.

However, some days you might want to explore on your own with the clay. You can make working with clay more enjoyable for both of you if you begin with an image for your child to focus on. For instance, by telling an exciting story beforehand, you can put your child in the realm of castles and dragons, just waiting to be given form. Or perhaps you can tell your child how much you'd like a little bowl to keep something in (buttons, paper clips, etc.). However you choose to do it, provide an image to turn into form.

As you begin to explore with clay, it may help you to have the image of a sculptor drawing the form out of a marble block. In one sense, the form is already contained within the ball of clay—it is your goal to slowly draw out the form. As you work with the clay, pushing, pulling, and squeezing it as its form takes shape, you might want to tell a story to your child about the form. You might say, for instance, "This lump here feels like it could be a fox's head, and I can feel the ears just poking out as two little points." (You will be creating these shapes as you talk.) "The body needs to be a little longer, and then the tail streams out behind . . ." At other times, you might want to present an image ahead of time, and work together in companionable silence. By working on your own creations at the same time, you can share the experience with your child and be on hand if any questions arise.

Once you have several completed pieces that your child wants to save, try to locate a kiln in your area so you can have your child's projects fired. Usually, craft stores can tell you where you can have clay projects fired in a kiln. If your local store does not have an available kiln, check online for pottery shops or local potters. Another possibility is to check with the local schools. They will often fire your objects for a small fee, if they have a kiln available. If not, they may be able to lead you to someone else.

Arranging for the use of a kiln will immeasurably enrich your child's experience with clay. There are more possibilities for projects of a practical, useful nature if they can be glazed and fired, which makes them able to withstand contact with water. When you inquire about a kiln, you should also learn about glazing, and the different glazes available. In addition to sealing the piece against water, glazes can add color, glossy finishes, and many other effects that can bring a greater beauty to your child's work.

Guidelines for Handcrafting

Handcrafts, such as knitting and crocheting, are exceptional activities for integrating thoughts, feelings, and actions. They can be tremendously harmonizing and satisfying.

Handcrafting requires us to enter into repetitious activity in a smooth rhythmical manner. It is important to continue on even when you have made a mistake. If you know how to correct your mistake and can do so, by all means do, but if you don't have the expertise at this time, don't stop or start over, simply continue working. Getting into the habit of making purposeful progress on a project will help deepen your awareness, focus, and rhythmical nature.

There is a connection between the outer form that you create and your inner state. Of course, this is true of all activities, but there are some activities that reflect this connection more clearly and accurately than others. Watch carefully the form that your crocheting and knitting take, particularly whether it is loose, very tight, whether your stitches are consistent, etc. At the same time, watch your inner states—your feelings, your thoughts, and your awareness of what you are doing. Did your own focus wander, or were you feeling tense while you knit? Use the feedback of the outer form of your knitting project to help you tune into your inner state and bring it into more balance.

As children learn handcrafting, this connection between the outer and inner state still applies, but we would never want to consciously force their attention on it. As parents and teachers, however, we can use this valuable information to help us work more effectively with our children.

Using Color in a Purposeful Way

It can be helpful to put some thought into the colors you select when handcrafting. The choice of color is usually an aesthetic one but we can become aware of how working with different colors affects us. Working intently with a certain color, particularly if that color is very strong and clear, can have a pronounced effect on your emotional and mental state. When handcrafting, we are often working with a single color for quite some time, as the project may take weeks to complete. By choosing certain colors, we can nurture the mind, body, and spirit. The effect of colors is an entire study in itself so we can't really go into it in much depth, but there are just a few principles that may help as you prepare to begin a new project.

Consider the qualitative value of the colors themselves. What feeling does each of the colors convey? Obviously, this is a very subjective experience. Some people find red to be uplifting and stimulating, for instance, and others find it puts them on edge. A lot of it has to do with your own temperament and needs: a fiery individual may feel an affinity for red because it reflects their own inner state, or may crave the soothing tones of blue and green to help balance this inner fire. And of course, this fiery individual could very well benefit from working with red at certain times and blue at other times. As always, a balanced life is the goal; using color gives us just one more way to achieve that.

So how does this help us in choosing colors for handcrafting projects? In general, colors are divided into groups: "warm" shades—reds, yellows, and oranges—are stimulating, and "cool" shades—blues, purples, and greens—are more soothing. Likewise, we can often see a general tendency in our own children (and in ourselves) toward either excitability or calm. Your own explorations with color will help you gain experience in determining how your child reacts to the different cool and warm colors.

As mentioned earlier, there are two ways to think about using color. The first is to select the opposite color from what we are feeling, to provide a balance to our inner state. For example, if we are feeling very excited, we might want to surround ourselves with the cool shades; this might help to calm us down. The second way to use color is as a reflection of our inner states, with the expectation that by having our inner state validated and nurtured by color, we will naturally want to embrace the opposite state in order to come into better balance. This opposite color will spontaneously arise within us. Think of it this way: if we are feeling angry or excitable and we surround ourselves with a bright red, we may soon reach inside ourselves to find a place of calm, to balance out all the excitement.

You can feel this phenomenon in an experiential way because our eyes naturally switch to a complementary color. To find the "opposite" (or complement) of a certain color, try this: Put the color you want to test on a white piece of paper and stare only at the color for about 30 seconds. Then, take the color away and stare at the white paper. You will see a color appear before your eyes, superimposed on the white paper, the exact opposite of the color you were just staring at. There are specific physiological reasons why this occurs (having to do with fatigue in the retina and rods and cones in the eye), but it reflects the color opposites found on a color wheel. This information can help us in our explorations of color. If you want to experiment with encouraging an inner experience of the opposite of a particular color (the second method for using color mentioned above), then the second color that you see when doing this experiment—the "nonphysical" color—is the color that will arise within you from using the original color.

Which approach is best for your child? There is no one right answer, of course, and you will probably find, through experimentation, that both seem to work at various times. However, by giving thoughtful attention to these principles, color can become a valuable tool in the learning process.

Finger Knitting

Finger knitting is an excellent activity for kindergarteners, and a great precursor to learning to knit. It is easy to learn and a child can make a long chain of finger knitting in a single session—very satisfying!

Purchase a skein of bulky yarn. The fat yarn is easier to manipulate and makes a nice, thick chain that can be used for a variety of projects. It is best for you to learn to finger knit first so you can teach your child without having to refer to the directions.

Once you have learned, start finger knitting when your child is around. At some point, they will probably become interested in what you are doing, at which point you can demonstrate how to do it and let your child give it a try. If your child becomes confused or can't do it right away, let it go until another time. Once your child gets the hang of it, you will have to decide what to do with all the long strings of knitting that are coming off your child's fingers!

There are many project possibilities. The finger knitted yarn can be coiled and sewn together to make pot holders or trivets, or it can be wrapped, then glued on cans or jars to make decorative holders. A longer strand or several strands can be coiled to make a small rug or a blanket for a dog's or cat's bed. Strands of finger knitting can be woven together (or looped back and forth and sewn together) to make a square or rectangular shape for place mats, a blanket for a doll's cradle, etc. You can also finger knit your finger knitting, or braid three strands together, to make a cord with an even bigger diameter. Whatever you choose to do with the final product is entirely up to you and your child.

A ball of yarn with a loose end

Loose end crosses UNDER

Loose end crosses OVER

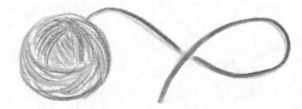

NOW, TO BEGIN

1. Make a slipknot in the yarn.

    Now it looks like this

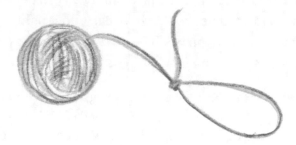

2. Sit in a chair

    a. Your left foot is next to the ball of yarn and holds it down.

    b. Your left hand holds the loose end up—vertical and taut.

    c. Your right thumb and forefinger are inside the loop, holding it wide apart and forming a triangle.

3. With right thumb and forefinger remaining inside the loop, grasp vertical yarn about one inch below slipknot.

4. While holding right hand stationary, pull loose end of yarn down with left hand until the loop slips snugly around the yarn. (Remember to keep your left foot on yarn.)

5. Continue holding the loose end with your left hand and pull up, letting loop slip on your right forefinger until it goes back to the size it was when you began step 3.

6. Put thumb and forefinger through loop, as shown in step 2, and then repeat steps 3, 4, and 5.

7. Adjust tension as you knit, so that the stitches are neither too tight nor too loose.

8. If you are left-handed, reverse "left" and "right" indications in the instructions.

Knitting

Knitting is a very practical skill to teach to children, not only in terms of what they can create, but in terms of helping them develop fine motor coordination. This is particularly beneficial for children who are just learning to write. Knitting strengthens their fingers and hands, and helps them become more aware of and in control of their hand and finger movements. This makes the physical act of writing easier and less fatiguing.

If you do not yet know how to knit, we have provided simple knitting instructions at the end of this section, but ideally you will be able to learn from someone who can sit next to you and show you first-hand. Knitters are usually happy to pass along their knowledge of this traditional craft. If you don't have a friend, relative, or neighbor who can teach you, check with your nearest yarn, fabric, or craft store. Once you learn the basics, you may want to get a book on knitting (check your local library or knitting store) to pick up helpful tips and great project ideas. You don't need to learn, nor teach, anything complex at this time. Casting on, the knit stitch, and casting off (or binding off) are all that you and your child need to learn for now.

When you have learned how to knit, practice a bit until you are comfortable with all phases of the process. If possible, use natural wool yarn, as this has a lovely feel to it and a resiliency that gives it good stretch and shape. Wool yarn comes in many different types, so choose one that feels soft and pleasing to you. Using large (fat) needles and chunky yard is helpful at first, for both children and adults. We recommend a No. 10 size needle for your child to use, so you may just want to get two sets of them. Wooden needles cost more than metal ones, but the yarn is less likely to slide off of wooden needles when you are working, which is also helpful for the beginning knitter.

If you would like to make knitting needles instead of buying them, this is a fun and simple project, and can be an excellent way to begin your child's knitting lessons. Buy dowels that are about the same width as No. 10 knitting needles (about $\frac{5}{16}$ of an inch), and cut them in one-foot lengths. Sharpen one end with a pencil sharpener. With sandpaper, sand them thoroughly, blunting the pointed tips and polishing the dowels meticulously so the yarn won't snag anywhere. This will require starting with quite rough sandpaper and progressing to finer paper. The finished needles will gradually become softer and darker as they are used because they absorb the natural oils from your child's hands. To prevent the stitches from sliding off the end of the needle, you can glue a fat bead on the end, or wrap colored rubber bands around the end until you have a fat ball.

Knitting Instructions

There are three steps you need to know to begin knitting: casting on, the knit stitch, and casting off (or binding off).

CASTING ON

METHOD 1

Never cast on too tightly. To begin casting on, make a slip-knot at a distance from the end of the yarn strand. To determine the length of this "free end" yarn, plan for about 1 inch of yarn per stitch for heavy rug yarn and large needles, and $\frac{1}{2}$" of yarn per stitch for lightweight yarn and small needles. You cast on by working the free end in with the ball yarn.

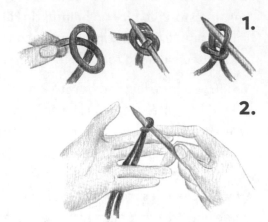

1.

Figures 1 and 2

Make a slipknot, place loop on needle and tighten.

Figure 3

With needle in right hand, insert left thumb under free end yarn. The yarn that is attached to the ball goes over the left forefinger. Hold this yarn taut by slipping it under the middle finger of the left hand.

3.

Figures 4 through 6

With left thumb, pull free end yarn out to form a loop. Insert needle into this loop and draw yarn through the loop, forming a new stitch.

 **4.**    **5.**    **6.**

Figure 7

With left thumb, pull free end yarn to bring the new stitch close to your needle. Repeat directions for Figures 3 through 7 for required number of stitches.

7.

METHOD 2

Never cast on too tightly. This method of casting on uses the knit stitch.

Make a slipknot, place it on the needle and tighten. (See Figure 1 in METHOD 1).

Figures 1 and 2

Hold needle in left hand, insert right needle into front side of stitch, front to back; bring yarn under and over right needle point. Draw yarn through stitch, forming new stitch. Keep stitch on right needle.

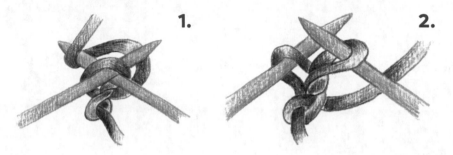

Figure 3

Insert left needle into front side of stitch, front to back, and slip stitch off right needle. Repeat directions for Figures 1 through 3 for required number of stitches.

HOW TO KNIT

1.

Figure 1

Hold needle with stitches in left hand. Keep yarn at back of work.

Figure 2

Insert needle into front side of first stitch, front to back.

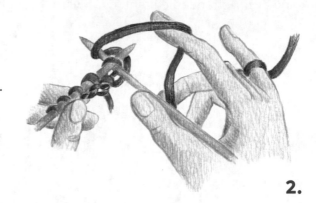

2.

Figures 3 and 4

Bring yarn under and over right needle point and draw yarn through stitch, forming new stitch.

 **3.**

 **4.**

Figure 5

Keep new stitch on right needle and slip old stitch off left needle. Repeat directions for Figures 2 through 5 for required number of stitches.

5.

Note: Be sure to keep each stitch to be worked near the tip of the left needle so it can be drawn off the needle easily when knit.

BINDING OFF

Figures 1 through 4

Knit two stitches. Insert left needle into second stitch on right needle and pull it over the first stitch. Repeat directions until one stitch remains. Pull first stitch over second and draw yarn through remaining stitch. Cut yarn, leaving an end of 2 or 3 inches to be woven into fabric with a tapestry needle or crochet hook.

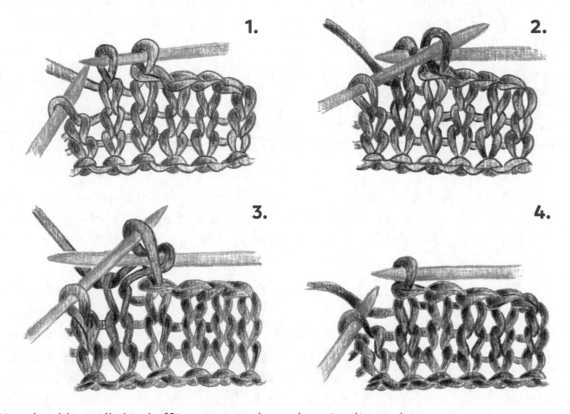

Note: You should usually bind off in pattern unless otherwise directed.

When your child is just learning to knit, it is helpful to sit together side by side, working on your own knitting. That way you can model good posture and technique, and be ready to lend a hand when your child drops a stitch, has a question, or forgets a step.

Here's a fun little rhyme that can help your child remember each step of the knit stitch:

In through the front door (the needle pushes into the loop)

Once around back (the free end of the yarn loops around the needle)

Peek through the window (the needle tucks back through the loop, bringing the yarn with it)

And off jumps Jack! (the new stich is slipped off the first needle)

If you notice your child's stitches are too tight or too loose, you can show how to increase or decrease the tension (something you will become used to doing in your own knitting).

After your child becomes more comfortable with knitting, you might want to read a story aloud during knitting time. Some children enjoy this while others get too distracted by the story and forget to knit. You can experiment and see what works best for your child.

First Knitting Projects

Your first knitting project should be simple and offer a chance to make mistakes without endangering the finished result. One project that we have found, which offers these possibilities, is a knitted ball that can be stuffed with cotton or cloth. This can be used later in games in the house, for its soft nature will not harm furniture or windows.

Start with enough stitches to make an 8-inch side and knit until you have formed a square (8 by 8 inches). Sew two sides together into a tube.

Then weave a length of yarn in and out of the stitches on the top edge, leaving extra yarn at the ends. Pull the ends of the yarn, gather the top edge together, and pull until it is closed. Then tie the string tight.

Fill the ball with cotton, wool, batting, or old pieces of cloth. After you have filled it, weave a length of yarn around along the bottom edge, gather it in the same way you gathered the top, and tie it off. Now your ball is complete!

Another excellent first knitting project is a small stuffed cat. Have your child knit a rectangle; the longer and wider it is, the bigger the cat will be. After casting off, fold the rectangle in half (this is how long your cat will be), and show your child how to sew the two edges together. You can use a large needle with a hole big enough for yarn, and your child can use the same color yarn to sew the sides. Then stuff the cat with a large amount of wool roving or cotton batting—you want a good, fat cat, so stuff the cat with as much as will fit in. The wool yarn will stretch as you stuff.

Sew the top edge together. Now you have a fat rectangular pillow. (You can stop here, if you'd like!) Take a colorful ribbon, and tie it around the cat's "neck"—this will create an indent that separates the head from the body. The two top points will now look like the cat's ears, and the two bottom points like its feet. Attach a length of finger knitting for the cat's tail. You can also sew on button eyes, or embroider dots for eyes, a triangle for a nose, and long whiskers. However, even a simple rectangle with a bow tied around it will easily be transformed into a cat in the child's imagination. Very little embellishment (if any) is needed. If your child liked this cat project, it can be fun to knit a whole family of cats and kittens, using different sizes of rectangles.

Don't be in a hurry for your child to finish a knitting project. As always, the benefit is not in the finished product, but in the process. Once you and your child know how to knit, you may find that one or both of you will occasionally take out the yarn and needles and quietly begin to knit, purely for the relaxing effects of the activity.

Crocheting

The first project is a scarf. This uses only the single crochet stitch and can be created in any size that will suit your own needs. It provides ample opportunity to practice on a broad flat pattern while refining the crocheting technique. In the beginning of crocheting, practice is what is most needed.

Start with a chain of stitches as wide as you want the scarf to be. Then, working back and forth with a single crochet stitch, build upon that chain, making the scarf longer and longer, until it is the length you would like it to be. A nice finishing touch is to loop several pieces of yarn through the ends of the scarf and cut them off neatly. It should look something like this:

Then tie the strands of yarn to group them together to form a tassel like this:

HOLDING THE HOOK AND YARN

You can hold the crochet hook in either of two ways. Both methods have loyal supporters who say that theirs is the best way. You'll have to try both and decide which is more comfortable for you.

1. Knife position. Hold the hook between thumb and forefinger as you would a knife. Rest the bottom of the hook lightly on the other fingers.

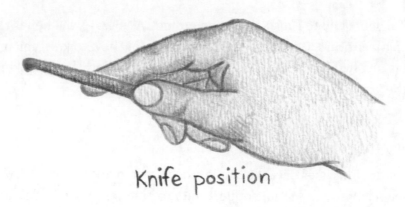

Knife position

2. Pencil position. Hold the hook between thumb and forefinger as you would a pencil, with thumb and forefinger on the flat part of the hook, keeping your middle finger forward to rest near the tip. Though this position gives you more control of the hook, it won't make your crocheting more efficient if it isn't comfortable for you.

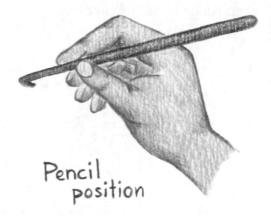

Pencil position

With your left hand, weave the yarn from the ball through your fingers as shown in either of the sketches below. Remember that the yarn always comes over your forefinger, from back to front, so that you can control its movement with your forefinger. You want the yarn to feed easily from the ball to the work with a consistent tension.

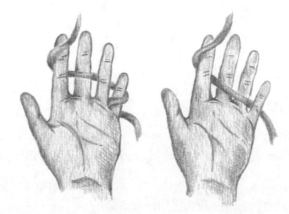

Use the middle finger and thumb of your left hand to hold the stitches you have made.

COUNTING STITCHES

Counting the number of stitches you have completed is more difficult in crochet than in knitting because the stitches are not left on the hook (the afghan stitch is an exception.) The numbers under the single crochet stitches in the following illustration will help you understand how to count them individually.

1 2 3 4

A BASIC RULE FOR CROCHET

For all stitches except the afghan stitch, always insert the hook under the two top loops of the previous stitch unless otherwise specified.

BASIC STITCHES

A

B

SLIPKNOT

You need to make a slipknot to hold your hook.

1. Several inches in from the end of yarn, make a loop. Hold the top of the loop between the thumb and forefinger of the left hand.

2. Place the long yarn end behind the loop and pull the yarn through the loop with the hook [**A**].

3. Pull yarn ends to tighten loop [**B**].

CHAIN STITCH (CH)

This simple stitch forms the foundation on which all crochet builds. Practice it (make a chain of 100 stitches or more) to gain a feeling for it and to develop stitches that are evenly sized and spaced. After you feel comfortable with the chain stitch, make a row of 20 chains to use as a base for the rest of your stitches.

1. Insert the hook into the slipknot.

2. Wrap the yarn around the hook, catching the yarn on the hook [**A**]. This is referred to as "yarn over hook." (YO)

3. Pull the yarn through the loop on the hook [**B**]. The "yarn over hook" and pulling of the yarn through the loop on the hook completes one chain stitch.

4. Repeat steps 2 and 3 until the chain is the desired length [**C**]. As you work, keep the thumb and middle finger of your left hand near the newest stitch to keep the chain from twisting.

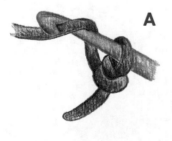

A

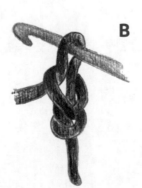

B

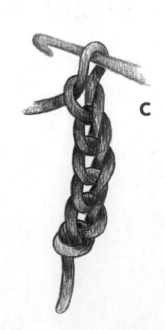

C

SINGLE CROCHET (SC)

The shortest of the basic stitches, single crochet is a tight stitch that produces a flat design.

1. Make a chain (CH) of any length (about 220 is good for a practice swatch.)

2. Insert the hook under two top loops (LPs) of second (CH) from hook.

3. Yarn over hook (YO) [**A**], pull yarn through (LP) on hook (2 LPs remain on hook) [**B**].

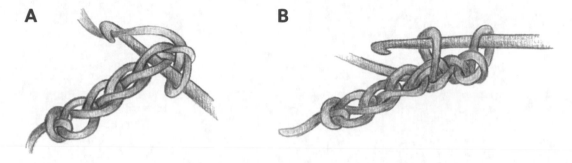

A **B**

4. (YO) and pull yarn through 2 (LPs) on hook. You have completed one (SC) [**C**].

5. Insert hook into next (CH), repeat (rep) steps 3 and 4. Work to end of row, (CH) 1 (always (CH) 1 at end of every (SC) row, except the very last row of your piece) [**D**].

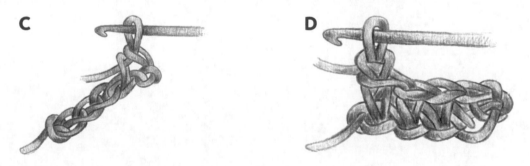

C **D**

6. Turn work (from right to left so yarn remains at back) to start next row [**E**].

7. On subsequent rows, insert hook in 1st stitch (st) of previous row [**F**]. Rep steps 3 and 4 to complete one (SC) in each (st) of previous row. (CH) 1, turn.

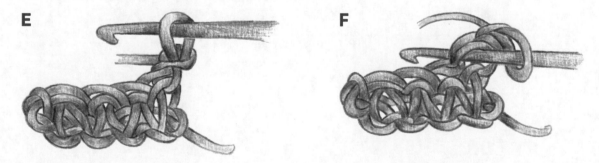

E **F**

ABBREVIATIONS TO LEARN

Chain Stitch	CH
Yarn over Hook	YO
Loop	LP
Single Crochet	SC
Repeat	rep
Stitch	st

Music Instruction

Music is an extraordinarily powerful element and has far-reaching effects in our lives. In many public and private schools, music is considered to be one of those subjects, such as arts and crafts, that is "nice" for children to have, but certainly shouldn't take too much time away from the "more important" academic subjects. This is unfortunate both for students and teachers. When children are introduced to music in a balanced manner, they will be able to use its great power to effect positive change in their lives. Music can become a powerful ally in teaching and learning, and an invaluable source of enjoyment, inner harmony, and self-expression for all students.

The most effective way that we have found to unfold the musical capabilities in young children is through imitation. If a home teacher tries, in a formal manner, to hold "music class," a child will often rebel against this. However, if that home teacher plays or sing songs for the feeling of joy or peace that they bring, this attitude will spread to the children present.

We encourage you to bring music into your home and your child's life in a variety of experiential ways, and enjoy together the harmony it brings.

Singing

Singing is one of the most important talents that a teacher can have. By developing this ability and gradually adding to the assortment of songs that are known by heart, it becomes an invaluable asset in working with children of all ages, and even with adults.

Choosing Songs for Children

When choosing songs for children, one must be very careful, for children absorb the wholeness of a song and do not discriminate as to the worthiness of that which is being absorbed. If a parent sings a popular song with a depth of feeling, the child is likely to imitate all of the subtleties inherent in the song, even if the parent is unconscious of them. If the song is full of feelings of despair, loneliness, or sexual longing, the child might later give voice to those expressive feelings, regardless of how adult they might be, complete with shocking innuendo. For this reason, it is best to select songs as consciously as possible, and only choose those that convey feelings that will be a source of strength to the child in their growth.

There are several factors to consider when choosing songs to effectively meet your child's needs. Songs for children, as with all songs, fall into several categories, and each type of song can be used for a specific kind of situation. For example, there are songs that open the heart, songs that activate the will, and songs that bring about a greater mental alertness. Some songs may help to calm a child who is anxious or angry, while other songs may help a bored child express a greater direction and purpose, while yet another song may help to uplift a child who is unhappy. As you use music in your parenting and teaching life, you will gradually begin to develop a feeling for which songs would be helpful in different situations. It helps to have many songs in your repertoire to choose from at any given time. The right song introduced at just the right moment can completely transform a child, or a group of children, and can turn impending disaster into an expression of joy in just a few moments.

However, in a very broad sense, it is helpful, in singing with children, to recognize the basic "polarity" of all songs, which is this: a song tends to either shift the focus of awareness outward or inward. Singing a song that shifts the awareness outward tends to make us feel lighter, more active, and increases our awareness of others. Singing a song that shifts the awareness inward tends to make us more thoughtful, introspective, and aware of ourselves. Both are necessary, of course, and one is not better than the other. It's just a matter of where you are and where you want to go. After you have sung countless songs countless times, you won't think about whether a song helps children go inward or outward, you'll just know instinctively what song to use for a particular situation.

Guiding Music Time Activities

In many situations, singing is a joint venture, without any particular motive, and it often includes lively action and movement. Singing (and moving!) is something that the parent/teacher and the children are doing together simply because they love doing it! There is a sense of cooperation and harmony as the musical experience is shared. However, sometimes, for a wide variety of reasons, the children are not cooperative and harmonious, and the energy in a room can become chaotic. When this happens, it is the teacher's responsibility to do something about it because that is part of what being a teacher is all about.

This is not always what teachers like to be doing because we all, teachers and parents, want to just relax and have everything go smoothly, so that we don't have to bring up something deeper from within us. It is helpful to remember that, in deciding to become a teacher, we have accepted the responsibility of helping others become more of what they are within, and this means that we have to become more of what we are within. Of course, it takes effort to bring a greater awareness and sensitivity to everything we do, and to help others do the same.

There are many ways to do this. Rather than attempting to force children to behave a certain way, try to work with the energy that is present, not against it. This is sometimes not easy at first, but with experience it will become more natural. To do this successfully, you must balance two polarities within yourself while you are in the midst of the activity. Outwardly, you must be moving with the children's energy, accepting them fully. However, inwardly you must be poised in the awareness of where they need to go to become more aware and sensitive, and use every opportunity to move them in that direction. It can be challenging to keep from losing yourself in the energy that is present! With practice, you can learn to be exuberant and active outwardly, while remaining poised and alert inwardly and using every opportunity to help the children move into a place of greater harmony. In this way, you can guide the lively music time in a purposeful direction.

When choosing songs for children, particularly when the energy is high, it helps to keep in mind the concept of working with the energy present, not against it. For example, suppose that you are working with your children, and they become very chaotic and scattered and you want to get them more quiet and focused. The usual tendency in such a situation would be to introduce a calming song. However, by introducing this type of song into a group of chaotic children you would not be working with the energy that is present, but against it. The children are likely to either ignore the song or get more silly and rambunctious. However, if you work with the energy present, you might introduce a song that involves a lot of activity, something with a lot of body movements (like "Here We Go 'Round the Mulberry Bush," with lots of skipping and marching around, for instance), for this will allow them to express the abundant energy that they feel. The song's strong rhythm will help to integrate them into one cohesive unit. After singing this song for a bit, you may notice the energy of the group begin to gain cohesiveness, and you will take your cue for the next song from the state of the group at that point. A song such as "This Old Man," demands awareness in order to remember the succession of words and movements; it can further corral the energy of the group. Thus, by working with the energy that was present at each step of the way, we gave the children opportunities to express themselves fully, and thus reach a point of greater sensitivity, harmony, and awareness.

Singing Tips

In addition to knowing how to choose a song and guide a music time activity, it is also important to feel comfortable singing. At this point, many people become very nervous and say something like, "I can't sing very well," or "I don't have a very good voice," or "I've never had any singing lessons." This makes not a bit of difference to your child. What matters most is your attitude of enjoyment and your willingness to learn.

However, there are things you can do to develop your singing voice. You may want to refer to the suggestions given in the storytelling section of this guide because many of those suggestions are relevant here. As with storytelling, it is important when singing to use your voice consciously to convey expression and presence.

When singing with children, singing a song "correctly" does not mean singing it with perfect pitch, or even hitting every single note. Of course, it is important to at least be "in the ballpark" as far as getting the notes right, but, perfection in regard to pitch or tonal quality is not nearly as important as the quality of energy you convey through the song. It is the attitude and presence you bring to the song that will help to encourage focus, disperse frustration, and inspire children to greater heights.

Try to forget, if only for that moment, all your insecurities, self-consciousness, fears, frustrations, doubts, and woes, and throw yourself fully into the act of singing. Bring as much strength, joy, and energy as possible into each note you sing. In this way, the songs will have the best possible effect on the children, as well as on yourself.

If singing or directing music time is challenging for you at first, you might find these tips and reflections helpful:

1. Listen to a tape of children's songs (such as *Oak Meadow Circle Time Songs*). Which songs do you feel appeal to the emotional life of a child? Which songs appeal to the development of a child's will or determination? Which songs might be helpful for focusing a scattered or overactive child?

2. After singing songs with your child, reflect on the experience. Did your child stay engaged throughout the music time? If their attention wandered or the energy became too chaotic, did you notice what was happening at the time? Why do you think your child became disengaged?

3. How did you feel overall about the experience? If your experience was not as enjoyable as you might have wanted it to be, what do you plan to do differently tomorrow to make it better?

4. How do you feel about your singing? Do you find it difficult, challenging, or easy to sing? Do you get tired from singing, feel a constriction across your chest, or run out of breath? If so, you can put some awareness into keeping your throat, neck, and shoulders relaxed as you sing. It is not necessary to sing at the top of your lungs, even if you are singing a very lively song. You can work on pushing the sound out from your belly (diaphragm) to better support your sound without having to work so hard.

Singing is a heartfelt, life-affirming way to connect with others and boost emotional and physical health. Don't give up if things don't go smoothly at first! Singing can become a highly enjoyable part of your day that everyone eagerly anticipates.

Playing the Recorder

Learning to play a musical instrument requires different abilities than those for singing. In singing, the child gradually learns to focus the often unfocused will and to direct it through one specific channel, the voice. With the addition of a musical instrument, the ability to integrate the hands into this process is developed. The child becomes more aware of the movements of the body, and bringing the body increasingly under conscious control.

The musical instrument that we use in the Oak Meadow curriculum is the recorder, but you are welcome to substitute any musical instrument you like. The recorder is an excellent instrument for children to begin with. It is inexpensive, portable, and relatively simple to play, and as the child becomes more proficient, it can be used to play quite sophisticated compositions alone or with other instruments.

The type of recorder we recommend is a soprano recorder. It is small enough to fit comfortably in a child's hand, and its tonal range encompasses two octaves from middle C to high C, the range within which a child's singing voice normally falls. Soprano recorders are sold at most music stores, and some toy stores. For children who are just learning to play, a plastic recorder is quite sufficient. You can buy a wooden recorder later if you wish when your child becomes more advanced.

To help you learn to play, we offer Oak Meadow's three-book recorder playing series: *Beginning Recorder, Intermediate Recorder,* and *Advanced Recorder.* There is just enough music theory included in each book to get you started so you can read the simple songs that are included in the instruction section. Start at the beginning and progress through each book in order. They are designed to be used with first, second, and third grade, using one book per year.

Practice a bit on your own first so you are able to support your child's learning. Trying to learn together at the same time generally causes too much frustration for the child or the parent. There are three main aspects of playing the recorder that will help you as you learn: breath control, tongue control, and finger placement.

Clear notes are produced by blowing gently but with a steady pressure. As you experiment, you will realize that blowing too hard causes the tone to become harsh and unmelodious. In addition, blowing too hard causes the individual notes to become a little higher (sharper) than the true pitch, just as blowing too softly will cause the notes to be lower (flatter) than their true pitch. If the breath is steady, the notes will sound as they should.

The next point to remember is tongue control. When you play, your tongue should behave in such a way as to give a clear and distinct start and stop to each note. The easiest way to do this is to use your tongue on each note as you would if you were saying "du-du-du." Try this a few times and you will see that when you do this, your tongue automatically opens and closes the notes sharply, like a little gate. Once you are familiar with this, it will stop being a conscious effort and you will do this without even being aware of it. It makes a tremendous difference in the quality of the notes and in the control you have in your playing.

Last, take the time to develop a correct finger placement, using the fingering charts in the recorder book. Place the fingers so that the fleshy part at the tip (where the fingerprint is) rests firmly flat across the hole. The fingers should be relaxed and comfortable. Put just enough pressure on the holes to cover them securely, but not enough to be straining.

Also, develop a relaxed but upright posture when playing, and model this for your child. It is best, especially at first, to stand while playing. This will help the breath flow more smoothly as well as help you keep the recorder in the correct position.

Once you have begun learning how to play, and enjoy playing, your child will be very eager to learn because of the beautiful sounds you will be making and the enjoyment you express.

Tips on Teaching the Recorder

When your child hears you playing the recorder, they will likely become very interested and want to try it too. When this happens, demonstrate how to hold the instrument and how to play the B note. This is the easiest note to begin with because it requires only two fingers in the proper positions. From the very beginning, focus your child's awareness on the quality of the tone being created. Particularly notice the breath control. Demonstrate for your child the correct technique, which you can explain in a very simple way. It can be helpful to provide an image, such as, "Pretend there is a small flame at the very end of your recorder, like you might find on a candle. Blow hard enough to make the flame flicker and dance around, but not hard enough to blow it out."

As your child becomes accustomed to the correct breath control, introduce the idea of moving the tongue to separate notes. Finally, work on the placement of the fingers. Children's fingers can be quite small, and sometimes it is difficult for them to cover the holes completely, or to move their fingers quickly from note to note. With children, regular practice is usually the best teacher in this respect.

Keep in mind that there is no need to rush. When learning a musical instrument, consistency is most important. In the beginning, five minutes of practice each day will accomplish more than one hour of concentrated practice once a month. Try not to let your practice sessions become something that your child does out of a sense of duty; instead, have each session arise in an apparently spontaneous manner, with you playing the recorder for enjoyment.

There may be occasions in which you are playing and your child isn't interested. If that happens, just continue playing for a while, then put the recorder away. The greatest attraction for your child is your enjoyment of what you are doing, and the prospect of doing something enjoyable with you. If that isn't enough to draw them in, then there is no point in trying to force it.

When teaching your child the notes and songs in *Oak Meadow Beginning Recorder*, there is no need to mention the name of each note or anything about musical notation. There will be plenty of time to introduce these technical aspects once your child is comfortable with playing the recorder. The goal at first is to encourage, inspire, and nurture a love of music and of playing a musical instrument. As children begin to experience the joy and sense of accomplishment that come from playing an instrument, they will eagerly seek to expand their capabilities by playing more difficult songs, and later learning to read music themselves.

By helping children unfold their musical ability, you are giving them an opportunity to enrich their experience of life, and deepen their understanding of themselves. Such attributes of character extend far beyond the musical harmonies your children may create, and they will influence not only their lives, but the lives of many others, as they move toward becoming complete human beings.

Appendix

Tongue Twisters and Letter Rhymes... 63

Songs, Verses, and Fingerplays 69

Opening Verses for Circle Time.. 69

Closing Verses for Circle Time.. 70

Poems 121

Poems by Maud Keary.. 121

Poems by Edward Lear 138

Poems by Dollie Radford 142

Poems by Robert Louis Stevenson 149

Verses and Poems Especially for Grade 3.. 159

List of Songs, Verses, Fingerplays, and Poems 171

Verses in Alphabetical Order 171

Poems.. 173

Verses and Poems Especially for Grade 3 175

Tongue Twisters and Letter Rhymes

A

My dame hath a lame tame crane.
My dame hath a crane that is lame.
Pray, gentle Jane,
Do you have the same
As my dame's lame crane that is tame?

B

Betty Botter bought some butter
But, she said, the butter's bitter.
If I put it in my batter,
It will make my batter bitter.
But a bit of better butter,
That would make my batter better.
So she bought a bit of butter
And she put it in her batter
And the batter was not bitter.
So 'twas better Betty Botter
Bought a bit of better butter.

C

You make a proper cup of coffee
In a copper coffee pot.

Chris carries cute cats in a cozy carton.
Can you carry a carton of cute, cozy cats?

D

Daisies, daffodils, and dandelions
Dance and dip at dawn

Remember always when reciting these verses, precise speech is key! See how fast you can go pronouncing every single consonant.

E

Eager eagles eat eels each eve.

F

One flea flew as one fly fled.
Fly, flea, fly.
Flee, fly! Fled!

G

Gallant green gargoyles garishly gargled garlic
While gorgeous gadfly Gretchen galloped gloriously.
Gloriously galloped gorgeous gadfly Gretchen
While gallant garish green gargoyles gargled garlic.

Two gray geese in a green field grazing.
Gray were the geese and green was the grazing.

H

Hilariously happy hippos
Hang heavily by their hair
Howling and hooting hungrily.

I

I like ice cream and icicles on ivy.

J

John jumps joyfully,
Joining jolly Judith.

K

Kay kept a key in a kettle.
The kettle kept the key for Kay.

L

Little lumpy lizards love little leaps.

Leopards and lions love licking lollipops.

M

Miss Moppet meowed at the miniature mouse.

Many mumbling mice make midnight music merrily.

Millions of marvelous men marched up the mighty, misty mountain.

N

Nutty Ned never needed noodles.
Noodles Nutty Ned needed never!

I need not your needles,
They're needless to me,
For needing of needles
Were needless, you see.
But did my neat trousers
But need to be kneed,
I then should have need
Of your needles indeed.

O

Moses supposes his toeses are roses,
But Moses supposes erroneously;
For nobody's toeses are posies of roses,
As Moses supposes his toeses to be.

P

Peter Piper picked a peck of pickled peppers.
A peck of pickled peppers Peter Piper picked.
If Peter Piper picked a peck of pickled peppers,
Where's the peck of pickled peppers Peter Piper picked?

Q

Quick quails quacked
Quit, quails! Quick!
Queen needs quail quills for quilting.

R

Robert Rowley rolled a round roll round
A round roll Robert Rowley rolled round
Where rolled the round roll
Robert Rowley rolled round?

S

Swan swam over the sea,
Swim, swan, swim!
Swan swam back again,
Well swum, swan!

She sells seashells
By the seashore.

T

Tiny Tim's trumpet
Toots tootle tee tee
Tee tootle, tee tootle,
Toots Tim merrily!

U

The blue glue is fluid.
Fluid glue is useful.

Sue uses ruby fruit juice.

Uncle ducks under his umbrella
But mutts run in the rain.

V

Veronica of the valley has a very vivid violet veil.

W

How much wood would a woodchuck chuck
If a woodchuck could chuck wood?
He would chuck the wood as much as he could
If a woodchuck could chuck wood.

X

Extra exams vex and perplex extraordinary oxen.

Y

A yawning yellow yak
Had a stripe upon his back.
He yanked a yellow yo-yo
And put it back into his sack.

Z

Fuzzy Wuzzy was a bear,
Fuzzy Wuzzy had no hair,
Fuzzy Wuzzy wasn't fuzzy, was he?

More Tongue Twisters

Cows graze in droves on grass that grows on graves in groves.

Any noise annoys an oyster, but a noisy noise annoys an oyster most.

Michael and Moses have very keen noses and very fine hoses for watering roses.

Plug the tub, plug the tub, plug the tub, plug
Scrub the tub, scrub the tub, scrub the tub, scrub.
Plug and scrub, plug and scrub, plug and scrub the tub.

If you can fry flour fritters,
Come and help me fry four flour fritters;
But if you can't fry four flour fritters,
Don't come help me fry flour fritters.

Though the threat of thirst or thunder
Thin the crops or flood the wheat,
Thickly thrive the thorny thistles
Through the wet or through the heat.

Fifths are hard to say,
A nimble tongue they need,
And sixths and sevenths and eighths and ninths
Are very hard indeed.

Of all the saws I ever saw saw,
I never saw a saw saw like that saw saws.

Freckled fishes flirting, flitting
Flashing fast or floating free,
Flicking filmy fins like feathers,
Feeding from the foaming sea.

> Repeat all of these tongue twisters at least three times. These, like all speech exercises, should be spoken precisely. Repeat and speed up your pace as you go! You may find the children walking around the house at strange hours saying these verses to themselves. They are a lot of fun.

A tutor taught on the flute,
Tried to teach two young tooters to toot.
Said the two to the tutor:
"Is it harder to toot
Or to tutor two tooters to toot?"

She sells seashells on the seashore.
The shells she sells are seashells I'm sure.
If she sells seashells on the seashore,
Where are the seashore shells she sells?

The swiftly whirling mill wheel grinds the gleaming grain.

Songs, Verses, and Fingerplays

Fingerplays and other children's verses and songs can easily be adjusted by using finger puppets, as small dramas to act out with the whole body. They work well with a group of children too. Feel free to experiment and adapt these verses to suit you and your child.

Many fingerplays and verses present counting and other simple number stories involving adding and subtracting, such as when children hold up five fingers to show five frogs, and one by one the frogs go away, or when two blackbirds fly away and then come back. These early math games help establish a solid number sense, and their importance cannot be underestimated as learning tools for beginning mathematicians.

Children's verses also help foster a love of words, and can ease the transition into reading. Enjoy them daily as a part of your circle time, language arts activities, creative play, or any other time!

Opening Verses for Circle Time

1. Morning has come
   Night is away.
   We rise with the sun
   To welcome the day.

2. The sun is in my heart
   It warms me with its power
   And wakens life and love
   In bird and beast and flower.

3. With joy we greet the morning sun
   Shining light on everyone
   It shines in the sky, on land and sea,
   And fills me with light when it shines on me.

Closing Verses for Circle Time

1. Guide my hands, left and right,
   As I work with all my might.

2. Here we are with joyful hearts,
   Working well and working hard.
   Helping gladly, quick and bold,
   Bringing joy to young and old.

3. We are truthful, and helpful, and loving in trust,
   For our heart's inner sun glows brightly in us.
   We will open our hearts to the sunbeams so bright
   And we'll fill all the world with our heart's inner light.

Songs, Verses, and Fingerplays

A Diller, a Dollar

A diller, a dollar,
a ten o'clock scholar,
What makes you
come so soon?
You used to come
at ten o'clock,
But now you come at noon.

Aiken Drum

There was a man lived in the moon
(Make circle over head with arms)

And his name was Aiken Drum.

And he played upon a ladle, a ladle, a ladle
(Pretend to strum an instrument)

And his name was Aiken Drum.

And his hat was made of green cheese, green cheese, green cheese
(Make a hat with hands on head)

And his name was Aiken Drum.

And his coat was made of roast beef, roast beef, roast beef
(Point to arms and chest to show the coat)

And his name was Aiken Drum.

And his buttons were made of penny loaves, penny loaves, penny loaves
(Show the buttons)

And his name was Aiken Drum.

And his waistcoat was made of crusts of pie, crusts of pie, crusts of pie
(Point to chest and stomach to show waistcoat or vest)

And his name was Aiken Drum.

And his britches were made of haggis bags, haggis bags, haggis bags
(Point to pants)

And his name was Aiken Drum.

There was a man lived in the moon
(Make circle over head with arms)

And his name was Aiken Drum.
(Drop hands down)

All the Year

This poem by Sara Coleridge is an excellent verse for memorization.

January brings the snow, makes our feet and fingers glow.
February brings the rain, thaws the frozen lake again.
March brings breezes, loud and shrill, to stir the dancing daffodil.
April brings the primrose sweet, scatters daisies at our feet.
May brings flocks of pretty lambs, skipping by their fleecy dams.
June brings tulips, lilies, roses, fills the children's hands with posies.
Hot July brings cooling showers, apricots, and gillyflowers.
August brings the sheaves of corn, then the harvest home is borne.
Warm September brings the fruit; sportsmen then begin to shoot.
Fresh October brings the pheasant; then to gather nuts is pleasant.
Dull November brings the blast; then the leaves are whirling fast.
Chill December brings the sleet, blazing fire, and Christmas sweet.

Ants Go Marching

The ants go marching one by one, hurrah, hurrah

The ants go marching one by one, hurrah, hurrah

The ants go marching one by one,

The little one stops to suck his thumb

And they all go marching down to the ground

To get out of the rain, BOOM! BOOM! BOOM!

The ants go marching two by two . . . The little one stops to tie his shoe

The ants go marching three by three . . . The little one stops to climb a tree

The ants go marching four by four . . . The little one stops to shut the door

The ants go marching five by five . . . The little one stops to take a dive

The ants go marching six by six . . . The little one stops to pick up sticks

The ants go marching seven by seven . . . The little one stops to pray to heaven

The ants go marching eight by eight . . . The little one stops to shut the gate

The ants go marching nine by nine . . . The little one stops to check the time

The ants go marching ten by ten . . . The little one stops to say "THE END"

And they all go marching down to the ground

To get out of the rain, BOOM! BOOM! BOOM!

The Apple Tree

Here is an apple tree with its leaves so green.
(Stand tall and strong like a tree with arms outstretched)

Here are the apples that hang in between.
(Make little circles with each hand to show apples hanging)

When the wind blows, the apples will fall.
(With arms waving, show wind blowing and apples falling)

Here is a basket to gather them all.
(Hold arms in front like a basket to hold apples)

Autumn

The leaves are floating gently down,
(Wave arms up and down showing leaves floating)

They make a soft bed on the ground. Then WHOOOO!
(Wave arms wildly, showing wind)

The wind comes whistling by,
And sends them dancing back to the sky.
(Hands flutter and dance showing leaves being lifted up)

The Beehive

(Do this first with one hand and then the other)

Here is the beehive,
(Hold fist closed with fingers inside)

Where are the bees?
Hidden away where nobody sees.
Watch and you'll see them come out of the hive.
(Watch closely to see them coming)

One, two, three, four, five!
(Creep the fingers out slowly while counting one at a time)

Bingo

There was a farmer had a dog and Bingo was his name-o
B-I-N-G-O, B-I-N-G-O, B-I-N-G-O
And Bingo was his name-o.
There was a farmer had a dog and Bingo was his name-o
(Clap)-I-N-G-O, (Clap)-I-N-G-O, (Clap)-I-N-G-O
And Bingo was his name-o.
There was a farmer had a dog and Bingo was his name-o
(Clap)-(Clap)-N-G-O, (Clap)-(Clap)-N-G-O, (Clap)-(Clap)-N-G-O
And Bingo was his name-o.
(Continue replacing letters with claps until you are clapping five times to replace the five letters)

Bow-Wow

Bow-wow, says the dog;
Mew, mew, says the cat;
Grunt, grunt, goes the hog;
And squeak, goes the rat.
Tu-whu, says the owl;
Caw, caw, says the crow;
Quack, quack, says the duck;
And moo, says the cow.

Chickens

Chickens are fun to imitate—enjoy!

Come and watch the clucking chickens as they search for things to eat.
They chirp and chatter cheerily and scratch about their feet.
From the garden patch and wayside ditch, as much as they can catch,
They eat and then each other chase, a choicer bit to snatch!

Chip, Chop

Pronunciation is key in speech exercises. When you model these for your child, feel free to exaggerate the consonants, particularly those at the ends of words. Children have a wonderful time with exaggerated speech!

Chip, chop, chip, chop! The woodsman with his chopper chops.
Chip, chop, chip, chop! Stout and strong and proper chops.
On beeches, oaks, and birches too, his hatchet gaily rings,
As he chops so cheerily, as cheerily he sings.

Chubby Little Snowman

A chubby little snowman had a carrot nose.
(Show long nose with closed fist like a trumpet in front of face)

Along came a bunny, and what do you suppose?
(Hands show the bunny hopping)

That hungry little bunny, looking for his lunch,
(Wiggle nose like a bunny)

Ate the snowman's carrot nose,
Nibble, nibble, crunch!
(Pretend to eat the carrot)

Clap with Me, One, Two, Three

(Do all the hand motions while speaking—try using the body as much as possible!)

Clap with me, one, two, three
Clap, clap, clap, just like me.
Shake with me, one, two, three
Shake, shake, shake, just like me.
Roll with me, one, two, three,
Roll, roll, roll, just like me.
Snap with me, one, two, three,
Snap, snap, snap, just like me.
Fold with me, one, two, three,
Now let them rest so quietly.

The Cobbler and the Mouse

(This is a delightful little tale. It can be used as a finger
play or a puppet play for which you use either gestures
or small hand puppets to depict the characters. The
child can also perform this verse with movement,
acting out the washing, tidying, and mending.)

There once lived a cobbler and he was so wee
He lived in a hole in a very big tree
He had a good neighbor and she was a mouse
She did his wee washing and tidied his house
Each morning at seven he heard a wee tap
And in walked the mouse in her apron and cap
She lit a small fire and fetched a wee broom
And she swept and she polished his little tree room
To take any wages, she always refused
So the cobbler said thank you by mending her shoes.

Daffy-Down-Dilly

Daffy-Down-Dilly has come up to town,
In a yellow petticoat, and a green gown.

Did You Ever See a Lassie?

Did you ever see a lassie, a lassie, a lassie?
Did you ever see a lassie go this way and that?
(Sway side to side, or pretend to be swirling a skirt)

Go this way and that way
And this way and that way,
Did you ever see a lassie go this way and that?

Did you ever see a laddie, a laddie, a laddie?
Did you ever see a laddie go this way and that?
(Sway side to side, or pretend to be high stepping)

Go this way and that way
And this way and that way,
Did you ever see a laddie go this way and that?

Diddle Diddle Dumpling

Diddle diddle dumpling, my son John,
Went to bed with his breeches on,
One shoe off and one shoe on;
Diddle diddle dumpling, my son John.

Doctor Foster Went to Gloucester

(*Gloucester* rhymes with *Foster*)

Doctor Foster went to Gloucester,
In a shower of rain;
He stepped in a puddle, up to the middle,
And never went there again.

Donkey, Donkey

Donkey, donkey, old and gray,
(Walk slowly, bending over lazily)

Open your mouth and gently bray.
(Exaggerate the "O" for open, with mouth wide)

Lift your ears
(Put hands on top of head to show ears)

and blow your horn,
(Cup mouth like a horn)

To wake the world
(Quickly raise hands above head and spread arms wide)

this sleepy morn.

Down by the Station

Down by the station
Early in the morning
See the little chuffer bellies
All in a row.
See the station master
Pull a little handle
Puff! Puff! Toot! Toot!
Off we go!

Elizabeth, Elspeth, Betsey, and Bess

Elizabeth, Elspeth, Betsey, and Bess,
They all went together to seek a bird's nest;
They found a bird's nest with five eggs in,
They all took one, and left four in.

The Family

This is my father,
(Point to thumb and wiggle it)

This is my mother,
(Point to index finger and wiggle it)

This is my brother tall;
(Point to middle finger and wiggle it)

This is my sister,
(Point to ring finger and wiggle it)

This is the baby,
(Point to little finger and wiggle it)

And oh, how we love them all!
(Clasp hands together)

The Farmer Plants the Seeds

(Sing to tune of "The Farmer in the Dell")

The farmer plants the seeds,
(Stoop and pretend to plant seeds in rows)

The farmer plants the seeds,
First the farmer plows the ground
(Pretend to guide a plow)

And then he plants the seeds.
(Stoop and pretend to plant seeds in rows)

The sun comes out to shine,
(Raise arms over head in a circle with hands spread like the sun)

The sun comes out to shine,
When the sky is very blue,
The sun comes out to shine.

The rain begins to fall,
(Wiggle hands in air simulating rain coming down, fluttering hands up and down)

The rain begins to fall,
When the clouds are in the sky,
The rain begins to fall.

The seeds begin to grow,
(Squat down and rise, using arms and hands to show plants growing up from the soil)

The seeds begin to grow,
From deep within our Mother Earth,
The seeds begin to grow.

The harvest time has come,
(Move arms to show the cutting of the grain and picking of crops)

The harvest time has come,
When the farmer gathers the plants,
The harvest time has come.

We can have some food,
(Pretend to eat)

We can have some food,
When the grain is made into bread,
Then we can have some food.

The Farmer Plows the Ground

(Sing to tune of "Here We Go 'Round the Mulberry Bush")

First the farmer plows the ground,
Plows the ground, plows the ground,
(Make plowing motions)

First the farmer plows the ground,
And then he plants the seeds.
(Make sprinkling actions)

This is the way he plants the seeds,
Plants the seeds, plants the seeds,
(Move hands to show planting)

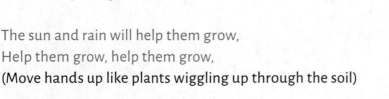

This is the way he plants the seeds,
So that they will grow.

The sun and rain will help them grow,
Help them grow, help them grow,
(Move hands up like plants wiggling up through the soil)

The sun and rain will help them grow,
Right up through the ground.

Now the farmer picks the grain,
Picks the grain, picks the grain,
(Hands make picking action)

Now the farmer picks the grain,
So we can have bread to eat!
(Pretend to eat)

Five Little Kittens

Five little kittens standing in a row,
(With one palm out, extend five fingers up and out)

They nod their heads to the children, so.
(Make the fingers nod)

They run to the left, they run to the right.
(Wiggle fingers left and right)

They stand up and stretch in the bright sunlight.
(Stretch fingers up high, slowly—reaching to the sun)

Along comes a dog who's in for some fun,
(Creep other hand toward the stretching fingers)

Meow, meow, meow!
See those kittens run!
(Run the fingers away to hide)

Five little mice sitting in a row,
(With one palm out, extend five fingers up and out)

They nod their heads to the children, so.
(Make the fingers nod)

They scamper to the left, they scamper to the right,
(Wiggle fingers left and right)

They stand up and stretch in the bright sunlight.
(Stretch fingers up high, slowly—reaching to the sun)

Along comes a cat, who's in for some fun.
(Creep other hand toward the stretching fingers)

Squeak, squeak, squeak!
See those little mice run!
(Run the fingers away to hide)

Five Little Monkeys

Five little monkeys
(Five fingers are held up)

Jumping on the bed.
(Five fingers jump on the palm of other hand)

One fell off and bumped his head.
(One finger falls off—child rubs head)

Mama called the doctor,
(Pretend to dial and speak on the phone)

And the doctor said, "No more little monkeys jumping on that bed!"
(Shake index finger and head to say "No!")

Four little monkeys . . .
Three little monkeys . . .
(Repeat until none are left)

Five Plump Peas

Five plump peas in a pea pod pressed,
One grew, two grew, and so did all the rest.
Grew and grew and grew and grew
And never, never stopped,
Till they grew so plump and portly
That the pea pod popped.

Five Speckled Frogs

(Continue from five down to one, demonstrating with the fingers)

Five green and speckled frogs,
(Hold up five fingers)

Sitting on a speckled log,
(Sit the fingers on the other hand)

Eating the most delicious bugs—yum, yum!
(Open and shut hand like a mouth)

One jumped into the pool,
(One finger jumps off)

Where it was nice and cool.
Then there were four green speckled frogs.
(Hold up four fingers)

Four . . .
Three . . .
Two . . .
One green and speckled frog,
Sitting on a speckled log,
Eating the most delicious bugs—yum, yum!
He jumped into the pool,
Where it was nice and cool,
Now there are NO green speckled frogs!
(Open both hands wide to show they are empty)

Fly Walk

Flies walk on the ceilings and straight up the walls,
Not even the littlest fly ever falls.
And I am quite certain if I were a fly,
I'd leave my home and go walk on the sky.

Footsteps

The foxes move so softly
That we don't hear a sound.
The trotting horses' hoofbeats
Ring out loudly on the ground.
And little lambs in springtime
Skip gaily round and round.

Friends

A little boy lived in this house.
(Make a fist with the right hand with thumb inside)

A little girl lived in this house.
(Make a fist with the left hand with thumb inside)

The little boy came out of his house.
(Bring the right thumb out)

He looked up and down the street.
(Move the right thumb back and forth slowly)

He didn't see anybody, so he went back inside his house.
(Hide thumb again)

The little girl came out of her house.
(Bring the left thumb out)

She looked up and down the street.
(Move the left thumb back and forth slowly)

She didn't see anybody, so she went back inside her house.
(Hide thumb again)

Then the little boy came out of his house again.
(Bring the right thumb out)

He looked up and down the street and all around.
(Move the right thumb back and forth slowly, and wiggle it all around)

Then the little girl came out of her house again.
(Bring the left thumb out)

She looked up and down the street and all around.
(Move the left thumb back and forth slowly, and wiggle it all around)

They saw each other.
(Point the thumbs at each other)

They walked across the street and shook hands.
(Touch the thumbs together)

They played together all through the day.
(Make the thumbs dance and play)

Then the little boy went back into his house.
(Hide the right thumb again)

And the little girl went back into her house.
(Hide the left thumb again)

From Wibbleton to Wobbleton

From Wibbleton to Wobbleton is fifteen miles,
From Wobbleton to Wibbleton is fifteen miles.
From Wibbleton to Wobbleton,
From Wobbleton to Wibbleton,
From Wibbleton to Wobbleton is fifteen miles.

Good Morning, Dear Earth

Good morning, dear Earth
Good morning, dear sun
Good morning, dear trees
And the flowers, every one.
Good morning, dear beasts
And the birds in the trees
Good morning to you
And good morning to me.

Grandma's Spectacles

Here are Grandma's spectacles
(Make circles with thumbs and forefingers and peek through them)

And here is Grandma's hat;
(Place hands on head with fingertips joined like a hat)

And here's the way she folds her hands
(Fold hands gently and place quietly in lap)

And puts them in her lap.

Here are Grandpa's spectacles
(Make bigger circles with thumbs and forefingers and peek through them)

And here is Grandpa's hat;
(Place hands on head with fingertips making a larger hat)

And here's the way he folds his arms
(Fold arms vigorously against chest)

And sits like that!

Hands on Hips, Hands on Knees

(Act out the words of the verse)

Hands on hips, hands on knees,
Put them behind you, if you please.
Touch your shoulders, touch your toes,
Touch your knees and then your nose.
Raise your hands way up high
And let your fingers swiftly fly.
Then hold them out in front of you
While you clap them, one and two.

Head, Shoulders, Knees, and Toes

Head, shoulders, knees, and toes, knees and toes
Head, shoulders, knees, and toes, knees and toes
Eyes and ears and mouth and nose
Head, shoulders, knees, and toes, knees and toes

Here We Go 'Round the Mulberry Bush

(Act out all the verbs—add your own verses!)

Here we go 'round the mulberry bush,
The mulberry bush, the mulberry bush,
Here we go 'round the mulberry bush,
So early in the morning!
This is the way we sweep the floor,
Sweep the floor, sweep the floor,
This is the way we sweep the floor,
So early in the morning!
This is the way we wash our clothes,
Wash our clothes, wash our clothes,
This is the way we wash our clothes,
So early in the morning!
This is the way we brush our teeth,
Brush our teeth, brush our teeth,
This is the way we brush our teeth,
So early in the morning!

This is the way we comb our hair,
Comb our hair, comb our hair,
This is the way we comb our hair,
So early in the morning!
This is the way we tie our shoes,
Tie our shoes, tie our shoes,
This is the way we tie our shoes,
So early in the morning!
This is the way we bake our bread,
Bake our bread, bake our bread,
This is the way we bake our bread,
So early in the morning!

Here's a Ball for Johnny

(You can use your child's name or any name in this verse.)

Here's a ball for Johnny, big and soft and round
(Make a circle with thumbs and middle fingers or with both hands together to make a bigger ball)

Here is Johnny's hammer, oh, how it does pound!
(Hammer with one clenched fist over the other)

Here is Johnny's music, clapping, clapping so!
(Clap hands together)

Here are Johnny's toys, standing in a row!
(Hold out hands with fingers outstretched, pointing upward with palms forward)

Here is Johnny's trumpet, toot-too-too-too-too!
(Hold hands like a trumpet in front of mouth)

Here's how Johnny plays peek-a-boo.
(Cover and uncover eyes with hands)

Here's a big umbrella to keep our Johnny dry.
(Hold forefinger vertical and place horizontal palm of other hand over it, making an umbrella, or put both hands over head like an umbrella)

It's time for Johnny to go to sleep, so we say bye-bye!
(Place palms together at side of head to show sleeping, and then wave bye-bye)

Hey, Diddle, Diddle!

Hey, diddle, diddle!
The cat and the fiddle,
The cow jumped
Over the moon;
The little dog laughed
To see such sport,
And the dish ran away
With the spoon.

Hickory, Dickory, Dock!

Hickory, dickory, dock!
(Move upright fingers back and forth in "tick-tock" motion)

The mouse ran up the clock;
(Both hands can be the mouse running up the clock, wiggling the fingers as the child raises the hands up)

The clock struck one,
(Stick one finger of each hand up to show "one")

The mouse did run,
(Have the mouse run back down, lowering the wiggling fingers)

Hickory, dickory, dock.
(Move upright fingers back and forth in "tick-tock" motion)

Home on the Range

Oh give me a home where the buffalo roam,
Where the deer and the antelope play,
Where seldom is heard a discouraging word,
And the skies are not cloudy all day.
Chorus
Home, home on the range,
Where the deer and the antelope play,
Where seldom is heard a discouraging word,
And the skies are not cloudy all day.

Where the air is so pure, and the zephyrs so free,
The breezes so balmy and light,
That I would not exchange my home on the range,
For all of the cities so bright.
Repeat chorus

Hoppity, Hop

Christopher Robin goes
Hoppity, hoppity,
Hoppity, hoppity, hop.
Whenever I tell him
Politely to stop it, he
Says he can't possibly stop.
That's why he always goes
Hoppity, hoppity,
Hoppity, hoppity, hop.

Hot Cross Buns!

Hot cross buns!
Hot cross buns!
One a penny, two a penny,
Hot cross buns!
If you have no daughters,
Give them to your sons:
One a penny, two a penny,
Hot cross buns!

How Far Is It to Babylon?

How far is it to Babylon?
Threescore miles and ten.
Can I get there by candlelight?
Yes, and back again.

Humpty Dumpty

Humpty Dumpty
Sat on a wall,
Humpty Dumpty
Had a great fall;
All the King's horses
And all the King's men
Couldn't put Humpty together again.

I Am a Fine Musician

I am a fine musician, I travel 'round the world.
I can play my violin, my violin, my violin.
(Extend one arm for a violin, and move the other hand back and forth against the "strings")

I can play my violin, fiddle-dee-dee-da!

I am a fine musician, I travel 'round the world.
I can blow my trumpet, my trumpet, my trumpet.
(Place hands at mouth like a trumpet)

I can blow my trumpet, toot-toot-toot-toot-toot!

I am a fine musician, I travel 'round the world.
I can crash my cymbals, my cymbals, my cymbals,
(Crash hands together, brushing up and down like cymbals)

I can crash my cymbals, crash-crash-crash-crash-bang!

I am a fine musician, I travel 'round the world.
I can beat my big loud drum, big loud drum, big loud drum,
(Pretend to beat drum or beat a real one!)

I can beat my big loud drum, boom-boom-boom-boom-boom.

I Had a Little Nut Tree

I had a little nut tree, nothing would it bear
But a silver nutmeg and a golden pear;
The King of Spain's daughter came to visit me,
All on account of my little nut tree.

I Saw a Ship a-Sailing

I saw a ship a-sailing,
A-sailing on the sea;
And, oh! it was all laden
With pretty things for thee!
There were comfits in the cabin,
And apples in the hold;
The sails were made of silk,
And the masts were made of gold.
The captain was a duck,
With a packet on his back;
And when the ship began to move,
The captain said, "Quack! quack!"

I See the Moon

I see the moon and the moon sees me
Over the leaves of the old oak tree
Please let the light that shines on me
Shine on the ones I love
Over the mountains
Over the sea
Back where my heart
Is longing to be
Please let the light that shines on me
Shine on the ones I love

I'm a Little Teapot

I'm a little teapot,
(Put right hand on hip, left hand extended with palm up)

Short and stout.
(Bounce gently up and down, flexing knees)

Here is my handle,
(Lift right hand from hip and replace it, showing the handle)

And here is my spout.
(Extend left hand farther and return to original extension, indicating the spout)

When I get all steamed up,
Then I shout
"Tip me over and pour me out!"
(Bend to the left, "pouring" out the tea)

I'm a very clever teapot, it is true!
(Put right hand on hip, left hand extended with palm up)

Here's an example of what I can do.
(Bounce gently up and down, flexing knees)

I can change my handle and change my spout.
(Switch right and left hands, changing sides for the spout and handle)

Just tip me over and pour me out!
(Bend to the right, "pouring" out the tea)

I've Been Working on the Railroad

I've been working on the railroad
All the live long day
I've been working on the railroad
Just to pass the time away
Can't you hear the whistle blowing
Rise up so early in the morn
Don't you hear the captain shouting
Dinah, blow your horn!
Dinah, won't you blow
Dinah, won't you blow
Dinah, won't you blow your ho-o-orn
Dinah, won't you blow
Dinah, won't you blow

Dinah, won't you blow your horn
Someone's in the kitchen with Dinah
Someone's in the kitchen I kno-o-ow
Someone's in the kitchen with Dinah
Strumming on the old banjo, and singing
Fee fi fiddly i o
Fee fi fiddly i o-o-o-o
Fee fi fiddly i oooooo!
Strumming on the old banjo!

If All the World Were Paper

If all the world were paper,
And all the sea were ink;
If all the trees were bread and cheese,
How should we do for drink?

If You're Happy and You Know It

(Act out the words, and add your own!)

If you're happy and you know it,
Clap your hands.
If you're happy and you know it,
Clap your hands.
If you're happy and you know it,
Then your face will surely show it,
If you're happy and you know it,
Clap your hands.
If you're sad and you know it,
Cry some tears,
If you're sad and you know it,
Cry some tears,
If you're sad and you know it,
Then your face will surely show it,
If you're sad and you know it,
Cry some tears.
If you're angry and you know it,
Stomp your feet,
If you're angry and you know it,
Stomp your feet,
If you're angry and you know it,

Then your face will surely show it,
If you're angry and you know it,
Stomp your feet.
If you're silly and you know it,
Wiggle your bottom.
If you're silly and you know it,
Wiggle your bottom.
If you're silly and you know it,
Then your face will surely show it,
If you're silly and you know it,
Wiggle your bottom.
If you're happy and you know it,
Shout hurray!
If you're happy and you know it,
Shout hurray!
If you're happy and you know it,
Then your face will surely show it,
If you're happy and you know it,
Shout hurray!

In the Barn

(This can create an entire farm in your living room. Add sound and movement fit to fill a barn.)

One black horse standing by the gate,
Two plump cats eating from the plate,
Three big goats kicking up their heels,
Four pink pigs full of grunts and squeals,
Five white cows coming slowly home,
Six small chicks starting off to roam.
Seven sweet doves perched upon the shed,
Eight gray geese waiting to be fed,
Nine little lambs full of frisky fun,
Ten brown bees buzzing in the sun.

Itsy Bitsy Spider

The itsy bitsy spider climbed up the waterspout.
Down came the rain and washed the spider out.
Out came the sun and dried up all the rain,
And the itsy bitsy spider climbed up the spout again.

Jack and Jill

Jack and Jill went up the hill
To fetch a pail of water;
Jack fell down and broke his crown
And Jill came tumbling after.
Up Jack got and off did trot,
As fast as he could caper,
To old Dame Dob who patched his nob
With vinegar and brown paper.

Jack Be Nimble

Jack be nimble, Jack be quick,
(Thumb of left hand is used as candle; index and third finger of right hand walk toward candle and jump over it)

Jack jump over the candlestick.
(Child can also jump, pretending to be Jack)

Jack Sprat

Jack Sprat could eat no fat,
His wife could eat no lean,
And so between them both, you see,
They licked the platter clean.
Jack ate all the lean,
His wife ate all the fat,
The bone they picked it clean,
Then gave it to the cat.

Kookaburra

Kookaburra sits in the old gum tree
Merry, merry king of the woods is he
Laugh, kookaburra, laugh, kookaburra
Gay your life must be!
Kookaburra sits in the old gum tree,
Eating all the gumdrops he can see.
Stop, kookaburra, stop, kookaburra
Leave some there for me.
Kookaburra sits in the old gum tree,
Counting all the monkeys he can see.
Wait, kookaburra, wait, kookaburra
That's not a monkey, that's me!

Lavender's Blue

Lavender's blue, dilly, dilly,
Lavender's green;
When I am king, dilly, dilly,
You shall be queen.
Call up your men, dilly, dilly,
Set them to work,
Some to the plough, dilly, dilly,
Some to the cart.
Some to make hay, dilly, dilly,
Some to thresh corn,
While you and I, dilly, dilly,
Keep ourselves warm.

The Little Bird

Once I saw a little bird go hop, hop, hop!
(Hop with the whole body or hop the fingers of one hand on the flat palm of the other)

And I cried, "Little Bird, will you stop, stop, stop?"
(Hold up hands like stop signs or shake index fingers)

I was going to the window to say "How do you do?"
(Pretend to shake hands)

But he shook his little tail
(Either shake your "tail" or wiggle fingers of one hand)

And away he flew!
(With hands, show bird flying away)

Little Bo-Peep

Little Bo-Peep has lost her sheep,
And can't tell where to find them;
Leave them alone and they'll come home,
Bringing their tails behind them.
Little Bo-Peep fell fast asleep,
And dreamt she heard them bleating;
But when she awoke, she found it a joke,
For they were still a-fleeting.
Then up she took her little crook,
Determined for to find them;
She found them indeed, but it made her heart bleed,
For they'd left their tails behind them.
It happened one day, as Bo-Peep did stray
Unto a meadow hard by.
There she espied their tails side by side,
All hung on a tree to dry.
Then she heaved a sigh, and wiped her eye,
And ran over hill and dale-o,
And tried what she could, as a shepherdess should,
To tack to each sheep its tail-o.

Little Boy Blue

Little Boy Blue, come blow your horn,
The sheep's in the meadow, the cow's in the corn;
But where is the boy that looks after the sheep?
He's under a haystack, fast asleep.
Will you wake him? No, not I;
For if I do, he'll be sure to cry.

The Little Ducks

Five little ducks went out to play
(Five fingers dance along like little ducks)

Over the hills and far away.
(Move fingers up and down, going over hills)

Mama Duck said, "Quack, quack, quack, quack!"
(Make "quacking motions" with thumb and fingers)

And four little ducks came running back.
(Four fingers come running back)

Four little ducks went out to play
(Four fingers dance along like little ducks)

Over the hills and far away.
(Move fingers up and down, going over hills)

Mama Duck said, "Quack, quack, quack, quack!"
(Make "quacking motions" with thumb and fingers)

And three little ducks came running back.
(Three fingers come running back)

Three little ducks went out to play
(Three fingers dance along like little ducks)

Over the hills and far away.
(Move fingers up and down, going over hills)

Mama Duck said, "Quack, quack, quack, quack!"
(Make "quacking motions" with thumb and fingers)

And two little ducks came running back.
(Two fingers come running back)

Two little ducks went out to play
(Two fingers dance along like little ducks)

Over the hills and far away.
(Move fingers up and down, going over hills)

Mama Duck said, "Quack, quack, quack, quack!"
(Make "quacking motions" with thumb and fingers)

And one little duck came running back.
(One finger comes running back)

One little duck went out to play
(One finger dances along like a little duck)

Over the hills and far away.
(Move finger up and down, going over hills)

Mama Duck said, "Quack, quack, quack, quack!"
(Make "quacking motions" with thumb and fingers)

But no little ducks came running back.
(Sadly shake head)

No little ducks went out to play
(Shake fingers and head sadly)

Over the hills and far away.
(Move fingers up and down, going over hills)

Mama Duck said, "Quack, quack, quack, quack!"
(Say it sadly, making "quacking motions" with thumb and fingers)

And five little ducks came running back!
(Say it happily, as five fingers come running joyfully back)

Little Jack Horner

Little Jack Horner sat in a corner,
Eating his Christmas pie;
(Pretend to eat)

He put in his thumb, and pulled out a plum,
(Stick thumb into opposite cupped hand or fist and pull it out dramatically)

And said, "What a good boy am I!"

Little Miss Muffet

Little Miss Muffet
Sat on a tuffet
(Semi-squat or act as if sitting down)

Eating her curds and whey;
(Pretend to eat)

Along came a spider,
And sat down beside her,
(Show the spider with wiggly fingers)

And frightened
Miss Muffet away.
(With hands, show her running away)

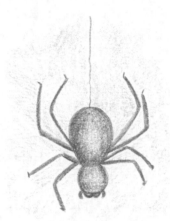

Little Mousie

See the little mousie
(Put middle finger and index finger on thumb to show the mouse)

Creeping up the stair,
(Creep the mouse slowly up the arm)

Looking for a warm nest
(Mouse is looking and snuffling)

There—Oh! There!
(Mousie wiggles into crook of elbow or armpit)

The Little Rabbit

Little cabin in the wood
(Make a pointed roof on head with both hands)

Little man by the window stood
(Peek through circled fingers)

Saw a rabbit hopping by,
(Make fist with index and middle finger pointing up like ears, and hop along like a rabbit)

Frightened as could be.
(Hunch shoulders and look scared)

"Help me! Help me!" the rabbit said,
(Raise hands quickly high overhead with each "help me")

"Or the wolf will eat me dead."
"Little rabbit come inside,
(Beckon with forefinger)

Safe with me abide."
(Fold one arm against the body and gently stroke as if stroking a bunny rabbit)

Little Robin Redbreast

Little Robin Redbreast sat upon a tree,
Up went Kittycat and down went he;
Down came Kittycat and away Robin ran;
Says little Robin Redbreast: "Catch me if you can!"
Little Robin Redbreast jumped upon a wall;
Kittycat jumped after him, and almost had a fall.
Little Robin chirped and sang and what did kitty say?
Kittycat said, "Mew," and Robin jumped away.

Lucy Locket

(Can be sung to the tune of "Yankee Doodle")

Lucy Locket lost her pocket,
Kitty Fisher found it;
There was not a penny in it,
But a ribbon round it.

Mares Eat Oats

Mares eat oats
And does eat oats
And little lambs eat ivy.
A kid'll eat ivy, too.
Wouldn't you?

Mary Had a Little Lamb

Mary had a little lamb, little lamb, little lamb
Mary had a little lamb
Its fleece was white as snow.
Everywhere that Mary went, Mary went, Mary went
Everywhere that Mary went,
The lamb was sure to go.
It followed her to school one day, school one day, school one day
It followed her to school one day,
Which was against the rule.
It made the children laugh and play, laugh and play, laugh and play
It made the children laugh and play
To see a lamb at school.

Minnie and Winnie

Minnie and Winnie slept in a shell.
Sleep, little ladies!

(Pretend to sleep, laying the hands together and resting head on them with eyes closed)

And they slept well.
Pink was the shell within,
Silver without;
Sounds of the great sea
Wander'd about.

Mistress Mary

Mistress Mary, quite contrary,
How does your garden grow?
With silver bells, and cockleshells,
And pretty maids all in a row.

My Bonnie Lies over the Ocean

My Bonnie lies over the ocean
My Bonnie lies over the sea
My Bonnie lies over the ocean
Oh, bring back my Bonnie to me.
Chorus
Bring back, bring back
Oh, bring back my Bonnie to me, to me.
Bring back, bring back
Oh, bring back my Bonnie to me.

Oh, blow the winds o'er the ocean,
And blow the winds o'er the sea.
Oh, blow the winds o'er the ocean,
And bring back my Bonnie to me!
Repeat chorus

My Maid Mary

My maid Mary, she minds the dairy,
While I go hoeing and mowing each morn;
Gaily run the reel and the little spinning wheel,
While I am singing and mowing my corn.

My Turtle

This is my turtle,
(Make a fist with the thumb extended)

He lives in a shell.
(Hide the thumb in the fist)

He likes his home very well.
He pokes his head out when he wants to eat.
(Poke the thumb out)

And pulls it back in when he wants to sleep.
(Hide the thumb again)

Nonsense Round

Don't put your dust in my dustpan, my dustpan, my dustpan,
Don't put your dust in my dustpan
My dustpan's full.
Fish and chips and vinegar, vinegar, vinegar
Fish and chips and vinegar, vinegaaaaaar . . . salt!
One bottle of pop, two bottles of pop, three bottles of pop, four
Five bottles of pop, six bottles of pop, seven bottles of pop, more.

Oats, Peas, Beans

Oats, peas, beans, and barley grow.
Oats, peas, beans, and barley grow.
Not you nor I nor anyone knows
How oats, peas, beans, and barley grow.

Old MacDonald

Old MacDonald had a farm, E-I-E-I-O.
And on his farm he had some chicks, E-I-E-I-O.
With a chick, chick here, and a chick, chick there,
Here a chick, there a chick, everywhere a chick, chick,
Old MacDonald had a farm, E-I-E-I-O.
Repeat using the following animals and sounds
Duck—quack, quack
Turkey—gobble, gobble
Pig—oink, oink
Cow—moo, moo
Cat—meow, meow
Mule—heehaw
Dog—bow wow

Old Mother Hubbard

Old Mother Hubbard went to the cupboard,
To get her poor dog a bone;
But when she got there, the cupboard was bare,
And so the poor dog had none.
She went to the barber's to buy him a wig;
When he came back he was dancing a jig.
"Oh, you dear merry Grig, how nicely you're prancing!"

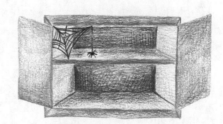

Then she held up the wig, and began dancing.
She went to the fruiterer's to buy him some fruit;
When she came back he was playing the flute.
"Oh, you musical dog! you surely can speak:
Come sing me a song!"—and he set up a squeak.
The dog he cut capers and turned out his toes;
'Twill soon cure the vapors he such attitude shows.
The dame made a curtsey, the dog made a bow;
The dame said, "Your servant;" the dog said, "Bow-wow!"

Once I Caught a Fish Alive

One, two, three, four, five
Once I caught a fish alive.
Six, seven, eight, nine, ten
Then I threw it back again.
Why did you let it go?
Because it bit my finger so!
Which finger did it bite?
This little finger on the right.

One Elephant Went Out to Play

(Can either be acted out with the whole body, one hand in front as the trunk and other behind as tail, lumbering along as an elephant—or as a fingerplay, with one hand as the spider web and the other using the fingers as the elephants.)

One elephant went out to play
On a spider's web one day.
He had such enormous fun
That he called for another elephant to come.
Two elephants went out to play
On a spider's web one day.
They had such enormous fun
That they called for another elephant to come.
Three elephants . . .
Four elephants . . .
Five elephants . . .
All the elephants went out to play
On a spider's web one day.
They had such enormous fun
But there were no more elephants left to come.

Another version builds on this verse:

One little elephant balancing
Step by step on a piece of string.
He thought it was such an amusing stunt,
That he called in another little elephant!

One, Two, Buckle My Shoe

One, two! Buckle my shoe.
Three, four! Shut the door.
Five, six! Pick up sticks.
Seven, eight! Lay them straight.
Nine, ten! A big, fat hen.
Eleven, twelve! Dig and delve.
Thirteen, fourteen! Maids a-courting.
Fifteen, sixteen! Maids in the kitchen.
Seventeen, eighteen! Maids a-waiting.
Nineteen, twenty! My plate's empty.

Open Them, Shut Them

(Do all the movements described in the verse, using hands, fingers, or any relevant body part.)

Open them, shut them, open them, shut them,
Give a little clap.
Open them, shut them, open them, shut them,
Lay them in your lap.
Creep them, creep them, creep them, creep them,
Right up to your chin.
Open up your little mouth
But...(long pause)—do not let them in!
Open them, shut them, open them, shut them,
To your shoulders fly.
Then like little birdies let them flutter to the sky.
Falling, falling, falling, falling,
Almost to the ground.
Quickly pick them up again and turn them round and round,
Faster, faster, faster, faster,
Slower, slower, slower, slower,
CLAP!

Over in the Meadow

Over in the meadow
In the sand in the sun, lived an
Old mother turtle and her
Little turtle one.
"Dig," said the mother,
"I dig," said the one, and they
Dug all day in the sand in the sun.
Over in the meadow where the
Stream runs blue, lived an
Old mother fish and her
Little fishies two.
"Swim," said the mother,

"We swim," said the two, and they
Swam all day where the stream runs blue.
Over in the meadow in a hole in the tree,
Lived an old mother owl and her
Little owls three.
"Whoo," said the mother,
"We whoo," said the three, and they
Whooed all day in the hole in the tree.
Over in the meadow by the old barn door,
Lived an old mother rat and her
Little ratties four.
"Gnaw," said the mother,
"We gnaw," said the four, and they
Gnawed all day on the old barn door.
Over in the meadow in a snug beehive,
Lived an old mother bee and her
Little bees five.
"Buzz," said the mother,
"We buzz," said the five, and they
Buzzed all day in the snug beehive.
Over in the meadow in a nest built of sticks,
Lived an old mother crow and her
Little crows six.
"Caw," said the mother,

"We caw," said the six, and they
Cawed all day in the nest built of sticks.
Over in the meadow where the grass grows so even,

Lived an old mother frog and her
Little froggies seven.
"Jump," said the mother,
"We jump," said the seven, and they
Jumped all day where the grass grows so even.
Over in the meadow by the old mossy gate,
Lived an old mother lizard and her
Little lizards eight.
"Bask," said the mother,
"We bask," said the eight, and they
Basked all day by the old mossy gate.
Over in the meadow by the old scotch pine,
Lived an old mother duck and her
Little duckies nine.
"Quack," said the mother,
"We quack," said the nine, and they
Quacked all day by the old scotch pine.
Over in the meadow in a cozy, wee den,
Lived an old mother beaver and her
Little beavers ten.
"Beave," said the mother,
"We beave," said the ten, and they
Beaved all day in their cozy, wee den.

Over the Meadows

(This is a lovely, lilting verse, perfect for a game of follow the leader. You begin and have your child follow, flowing through your home as streamlets. Then change places, and see where you end up!)

Over the meadows green and wide
Blooming in the sunlight, blooming in the sunlight
Over the meadows green and wide
Off we go a-roaming side by side, Hey!
Streamlets down mountains go, pure from the winter's snow.
Joining they swiftly go, singing of life so free.
Streamlets down the mountains go, pure from the winter's snow.
Joining, they swiftly go, calling to me!

The Owl

(This would be a fun time to practice hooting like an owl!)

The owl hooted and told of the morning star,
He hooted again and told of the dawn.

Oysters

An oyster met an oyster, and there were oysters two;
Two oysters met two oysters, and they were oysters, too;
Four oysters met a pint of milk, and they were oyster stew.

Pat-a-Cake, Pat-a-Cake

Pat-a-cake, pat-a-cake, baker's man,
(Clap hands together lightly)

Bake me a cake as fast as you can.
Roll it and pat it
(Pass hands over each other in circular motion as if rolling and patting
a cake)

and mark it with T,
(Form the shape of "T" in the air with a finger)

And put in the oven for Tommy and me.
(Outstretch arms as if putting cake in oven)

Peas

I eat my peas with honey,
I've done it all my life.
I know it may seem funny,
But it keeps them on my knife.

Peas Porridge Hot

(This can be done as a hand-clapping game.)

Peas porridge hot,
Peas porridge cold,
Peas porridge in the pot,
Nine days old.
Some like it hot,
Some like it cold,
Some like it in the pot,
Nine days old.

Pop! Goes the Weasel

All around the mulberry bush
The monkey chased the weasel
The monkey thought 'twas all in fun
Pop! Goes the weasel!
A penny for a spool of thread
A penny for a needle
That's the way the money goes
Pop! Goes the weasel!

Rock-a-Bye, Baby

Rock-a-bye, baby, on the tree top!
(Rock arms gently, then more vigorously, as if holding a doll or baby)

When the wind blows the cradle will rock,
(Rock a little more vigorously, swinging high and low)

When the bough breaks the cradle will fall,
(Gently lower the arms down, as if putting a baby in bed)

And down will come baby, cradle and all.
(It might be fun to actually rock a stuffed animal or doll during this verse)

Rumble, Blunder

Rumble, blunder, stumble, thunder,
Wrangle, tangle, jingle-jangle!
Fluttery, stuttery, bog, fog,
Missing his tack,
Changing his track.
Flash! Dash! Splash! Crash!
Slowly, fastly, grimly, ghastly,
Firstly, secondly, thirdly, lastly.

Rumbling and Rattling

(Beware! This is a loud one! Run through the house with a long piece of white silk flowing out behind
as the roaring wind. What fun!)

Rumbling up the chimneys! Rattling at the doors!
Round the roofs and round the roads the rude wind roars!
Raging through the darkness! Raving through the trees!
Racing off again across the great gray seas.

She'll Be Coming 'Round the Mountain

She'll be coming 'round the mountain when she comes, (when she comes).
She'll be coming 'round the mountain when she comes, (when she comes).
She'll be coming 'round the mountain, she'll be coming 'round the mountain,
She'll be coming 'round the mountain when she comes, (when she comes).
Repeat the same pattern with the following verses (feel free to make up more!):

She'll be driving six white horses when she comes, etc.
She'll be wearing pink pajamas when she comes, etc.
Oh we'll all run out to meet her when she comes, etc.

Simple Simon

Simple Simon met a pieman
Going to the fair;
Says Simple Simon to the pieman,
"Let me taste your ware."
Says the pieman to Simple Simon
"Show me first your penny;"
Says Simple Simon to the pieman,
"Indeed I have not any."
Simple Simon went a-fishing
For to catch a whale;
All the water he had got
Was in his mother's pail.
Simple Simon went to look,
If plums grew on a thistle;
He pricked his fingers very much,
Which made poor Simon whistle.
He went for water in a sieve,
But soon it all fell through;
And now poor Simple Simon
Bids you all adieu.

Sippity Sup

Sippity sup, sippity sup,
Bread and milk from a china cup.
Bread and milk from a bright silver spoon
Made of a piece of the bright silver moon.
Sippity sup, sippity sup,
Sippity, sippity sup.

Six Thin Things

I can think of six thin things, six thin things, can you?
Yes I can think of six thin things and of six thick ones too.

Skin-a-ma-rink

Skin-a-ma-rink a-dink a-dink
Skin-a-ma-rink a-doo
I love you
Skin-a-ma-rink a-dink a-dink
Skin-a-ma-rink a-doo
I love you
I love you in the morning
And in the afternoon
I love you in the evening
And underneath the moon
Skin-a-ma-rink a-dink a-dink
Skin-a-ma-rink a-doo
I love you (and you and you and you and you)
(Repeat as many "yous" as there are people present, pointing to each
person in turn)

Skip to My Lou

Skip, skip, skip to my Lou,
Skip, skip, skip to my Lou,
Skip, skip, skip to my Lou,
Skip to my Lou, my darlin'.
Flies in the buttermilk, shoo, fly, shoo.
Flies in the buttermilk, shoo, fly, shoo.
Flies in the buttermilk, shoo, fly, shoo.
Skip to my Lou, my darlin'.
Repeat the same pattern with the following verses:

There's a little red wagon, paint it blue, etc.
I lost my partner, what'll I do?, etc.
Cat's in the cream jar, ooh, ooh, ooh, etc.

Snail Song

(Drag out the words slowly)

The snail is s-o s-l-o-w, the snail is s-o s-l-o-w,
(Creep fingers along the arm very slowly)

He creeps and creeps along.
And as he does he sings his song
The s-n-a-i-l i-s s-o s-l-o-w.

Softly, Softly

(Use white silks for this verse. Children can dance as snow and gently settle to the earth. It is fun to have children lie on the floor and repeat the verse with you while you let the silk billow over and finally cover them.)

Softly, softly, through the darkness, snow is falling.
Sharply, sharply in the meadows, lambs are calling.
Coldly, coldly all around me, winds are blowing.
Brightly, brightly up above me, stars are glowing.

Teddy Bear

(Do all the actions the words describe.)

Teddy bear, teddy bear, turn around;
Teddy bear, teddy bear, touch the ground.
Teddy bear, teddy bear, show your shoe;
Teddy bear, teddy bear, that will do!
Teddy bear, teddy bear, go upstairs;
Teddy bear, teddy bear, say your prayers;
Teddy bear, teddy bear, turn out the light;
Teddy bear, teddy bear, say "Good night!"

Ten Little Fingers

I have ten little fingers,
(Wave all fingers high in the air)

They all belong to me.
(Point to self)

I can make them do things,
Would you like to see?
(On following verses do the actions mentioned)

I can close them up tight.
I can open them up wide.
I can hold them up high.
I can put them at my side.
I can wave them to and fro.
And I can hold them just so.
(Fold hands at waist)

There Was a Crooked Man

There was a crooked man, and he went a crooked mile,
He found a crooked sixpence against a crooked stile:
He bought a crooked cat, which caught a crooked mouse,
And they all lived together in a crooked little house.

This Old Man

(Use the form of the first verse for all subsequent verses.)

This old man, he played one,
(Hold up one finger)

He played knick-knack on his thumb.
(Tap both thumbs together)

With a knick-knack, paddy-whack, give a dog a bone,
(Tap knees, clap hands, extend one hand)

This old man came rolling home.
(Roll hands)

This old man, he played two,
(Hold up two fingers)

He played knick-knack on his shoe,
(Tap shoe)

With a . . .
This old man, he played three,
(Hold up three fingers)

He played knick-knack on his knee,
(Tap knee)

With a . . .
This old man, he played four,
(Hold up four fingers)

He played knick-knack on his floor,
(Tap floor)

With a . . .
This old man, he played five,
(Hold up five fingers)

He played knick-knack on his hive,
(Make a fist and tap other fingers on fist)

With a . . .
This old man, he played six,
(Hold up six fingers)

He played knick-knack on his sticks,
(Hold fingers of one hand out like sticks and tap with other fingers)

With a . . .
This old man, he played seven,
(Hold up seven fingers)

He played knick-knack up to heaven,
(Tap fingers upward)

With a . . .
This old man, he played eight,
(Hold up eight fingers)

He played knick-knack on his plate,
(Tap fingers on one palm)

With a . . .
This old man, he played nine,
(Hold up nine fingers)

He played knick-knack on his spine,
(Tap fingers on spine)

With a . . .
This old man, he played ten,
(Hold up ten fingers)

He played knick-knack now and then,
(Tap on closed fist)

With a . . .

Three Little Kittens

Three little kittens
lost their mittens,
And they began to cry,
(Mimic crying and wiping eyes)

"Oh, mother dear, we sadly fear
Our mittens we have lost!"
"What? Lost your mittens?
You naughty kittens!
(Shake finger as if chastising)

Then you shall have no pie."
"Meow, meow, meow, meow!"
"You shall have no pie!"
The three little kittens
found their mittens,
And they began to cry,
(Mimic crying and wiping eyes)

"Oh, mother dear, see here, see here,
Our mittens we have found."
"What? Found your mittens?
You good little kittens!
(Open arms and pretend to pat and hug kittens)

Then you shall have some pie."
"Purr, purr, purr, purr."
"You shall have some pie!"

Three Wise Men of Gotham

Three wise men of Gotham
Went to sea in a bowl.
If the bowl had been stronger
My song had been longer.

Three Young Rats

Three young rats with black felt hats,
Three young ducks with white straw flats,
Three young dogs with curling tails,
Three young cats with demi-veils,

Went out to walk with two young pigs
In satin vests and sorrel wigs;
But suddenly it chanced to rain,
And so they all went home again.

Tom, Tom, the Piper's Son

Tom, Tom, the piper's son,
(Simulate playing a tin whistle)

He learned to play when he was young,
But the only tune that he could play
Was "Over the hills and far away."
(Dance the fingers "over the hills and far away")

Twinkle, Twinkle, Little Star

Twinkle, twinkle, little star,
How I wonder what you are.
(Open and close hands to show the stars twinkling)

Up above the world so high,
(Slowly raise arms high overhead)

Like a diamond in the sky!
(Touch forefingers and thumbs together to make a diamond shape)

Twinkle, twinkle, little star,
How I wonder what you are.

Two Apples

Way up high in the apple tree
(Raise arms up high and make a circle with each hand to show apples)

Two shiny apples smiled at me.
(Show exaggerated smile)

I shook the tree as hard as I could,
(Pretend to shake the tree)

And down came the apples;
(Drop hands down one at a time)

Yum . . . mm . . . mm . . . were they good!
(Pat stomach in satisfaction)

Two Little Blackbirds

Two little blackbirds sitting on a hill,
(Both hands in fists with thumbs up
to show birds; bounce fists up and
down a little)

One named Jack, the other named Jill.
(Lift up one hand—Jack—and then
the other—Jill)

Fly away, Jack;
(Jack's hand flies away behind you)

Fly away, Jill.
(Jill's hand flies away behind you)

Come back, Jack;
(Jack's hand comes flying back and sits down)

Come back, Jill!
(Jill's hand comes flying back and sits down)

Two Little Hands

(Do all the actions in the verse.)

Two little hands go clap, clap, clap.
Two little feet go tap, tap, tap.
Two little hands go thump, thump, thump.
Two little feet go jump, jump, jump.
One little body turns round and round.
One little body sits quietly down.

Vintery, Mintery, Cutery, Corn

Vintery, mintery, cutery, corn,
Apple seed and apple thorn;
Wire, briar, limber lock,
Three geese in a flock.
One flew east,
And one flew west,
And one flew over the cuckoo's nest.

The Wheels on the Bus

(Act out the words, and add your own verses too!)

The wheels on the bus go 'round and 'round,
'Round and 'round, 'round and 'round.
The wheels on the bus go 'round and 'round,
All around the town.
The people on the bus go bump, bump, bump,
Bump, bump, bump, bump, bump, bump.
The people on the bus go bump, bump, bump,
All around the town.
The driver on the bus says, "Move on back!
Move on back! Move on back!"
The driver on the bus says, "Move on back!"
All around the town.
The money on the bus goes clink, clink, clink!
Clink, clink, clink, clink, clink, clink!
The money on the bus goes clink, clink, clink!
All around the town.

Other verses:

The windows on the bus go up and down, etc.
The doors on the bus go open and shut, etc.
The babies on the bus go, "Wah, wah, wah!", etc.
The mothers on the bus say, "Shh, shh, shh", etc.
The wipers on the bus go swish, swish, swish, etc.
The horn on the bus goes beep, beep, beep, etc.
(And end with verse one!)

Whirling Leaves

(Flutter the fingers above head and to the ground—over and over)

The little leaves are whirling round, round, round,
The little leaves are whirling round,
Falling to the ground.
Round, round, round, round,
(Begin to whisper, fluttering fingers round and round and down)

Falling to the ground.

Wiggling and Jiggling

(Act out all the action words.)

Frogs jump. Caterpillars hump.
Worms wiggle. Bugs jiggle.
Rabbits hop. Horses clop.
Snakes slide. Eagles glide.
Mice creep. Deer leap.
Puppies bounce. Kittens pounce.
Lions stalk. But I WALK!

The Wind

(This is a song by Marlys Swinger. It is meant to be sung or recited with a sway and a twirl. Get out your silks and see where the wind takes you!)

I can't see the wind but the wind can see me
It follows me dancing across Lantern Lea
It blows round my ankles
It puffs up my hair
It tangles me up till I do not know where
Or whither or thither or why I'm this way
The way of the wind on a merry March day.

Wise Old Owl

A wise old owl sat in an oak,
The more he heard, the less he spoke;
The less he spoke, the more he heard;
Why aren't we all like that wise old bird?

Poems

Poems by Maud Keary

(from *Enchanted Tulips and Other Verses for Children*)

The Alphabet

Long the Alphabet
In my blue reading book:
There is each letter set,
With its peculiar look —
Some seeming fat and glad,
Others a little sad.
Some seeming very wise,
Some with a roguish look,
Making all kinds of eyes
In my blue reading book!
While a few seem to say,
"Shall you know us today?"

A Beetle Tale

"O come," the elder beetle said,
"For every one is safe in bed,
"Tis time to seek our nightly bread."
Then forth he crept with stealthy tread.
The clock ticked on—you would not deem
Aught could have broke that peace supreme,
The children slept, they scarce did dream,
The young moon cast a fitful gleam.
From crack and cranny beetles crept;
In black and polished coats they stepped
Upon that floor, which Jane had swept!
Ah me! How fast those children slept!

The elder beetle scratched his head
And thought a moment—then he said:
"Follow me, children, and be fed."
Forth to the larder door he led.
The Cook turned in her sleep—too late!
She should have covered with a plate
The dish that none shall save from fate;
She dreams the clock is striking eight!
But ah! Not yet the night has run,
Not yet appears the morning sun —
Cook's handiwork is soon undone,
The tarts are eaten every one!

A Dream

Last night when I was fast asleep,
Who do you think ran after me?
But A, B, C, each holding hands —
It was the strangest sight to see!
A danced a jig on nimble feet,
Fat B sat down upon the bed,
And C, to show what he could do,
Turned round and stood upon his head!
In blank surprise I stared at them —
How odd the dancing letters seemed!
And then I rubbed my eyes and woke,
And knew that I had only dreamed!

A Fly

Come and see this busy fly
Rub his skinny hands together,
Now he stops and wonders whether
He feels clean again and dry.
Is it to the left or right,
The way back to the windowpane?
He thinks he'll go and dance again,
He feels so tidied up and bright!

A Snail

A snail crept up the lily's stalk:
"How nice and smooth," said he;
"It's quite a pleasant evening walk,
And just the thing for me!"

At Night

Silence and night were in the air,
I heard their whispers everywhere;
And wind-breaths through the wallflowers went
Like unseen bees in search of scent.
Deep in the sky some stars were burning,
And then—I heard the round world turning!

Beneath the Sea

Were I a fish beneath the sea,
Shell-paved and pearl-brocaded,
Would you come down and live with me,
In groves by coral shaded?
No washing would we have to do;
Our cushions should be sponges —
And many a great ship's envious crew
Should watch our merry plunges!

Birthdays

When birthdays come, we always write
Our names upon the nursery door,
And carefully we mark the height,
Each standing shoeless on the floor.
How strange to think birthdays will be
When we shall never add one more
To all those marks which gradually
Are climbing up the nursery door!

Blackberries

In the garden strawberries grow,
Where anybody may not go,
But blackberries grow by the road,
Where all may get a basket-load;
So, little children, take your fill —
Then carry homewards what you will.

Clouds

Curly clouds of snowy white,
Fleecy islands in the light,
Prettier than cotton-wool,
Come and be my bed to-night
E'en a king would not disdain
Golden cloud for counterpain,
White ones for the sheets so cool,
Pillows like a silken skein!
Oh! to sleep and dream, and wake
With the cloud's first morning shake,
Hear the broad Earth stir below,
Watch the shining daylight break!
Lying safe upon my cloud,
Feeling like a fairy proud,
Sailing softly I should go,
Singing like the larks aloud!

Cuckoo Flowers and Daisies

Cuckoo flowers and daisies,
Grasses grey with dew,
Sunbeams of buttercups,
And a sky all blue.
Primroses and cowslips,
Bluebells and sweet may,
And a cuckoo calling
Far, far away.
Forget-me-nots and cresses,
In the streamlet blue,
Fly a little nearer,
O Cuckoo, do!

Enchanted Tulips

Tulips white and tulips red,
Sweeter than a violet bed!
Say, old Mother Bailey, say
Why your tulips look so gay,
Why they smell so sweet, and why
They bloom on when others die?
"By the pixies' magic power
Do my tulips always flower,
By the pixies' magic spell
Do they give so sweet a smell!
Tulips, tulips, red and white,
Fill the pixies with delight!
"Pixy women, pixy men,
Seek my tulips from the glen;
Midnight come, they may be heard
Singing sweet as any bird,
Singing their wee babes to rest
In the tulips they love best!"

Fairyland

A fairy's house stands in a wood,
Midst fairy trees and flowers,
Where daisies sing like little birds
Between the sun and showers,
And grasses whisper tiny things
About this world of ours.
Such flowers are there beside the way,
Lilies and hollyhocks:
Blow off their stalks to tell the time
Tall dandelion clocks;
While harebells ring an hourly chime
Like a wound music-box.
Some day shall we two try to find
This strange enchanted place?
Go hand in hand through flower-lit woods
Where living trees embrace—
And suddenly, as in a dream,
Behold a fairy's face!

Stand Still and Watch

Stand still and watch the clock's grave face,
The hands go round an even pace,
The hands go round, and though so slow,
In vain we try to see them go!
But watch that long black hand again,
Did you not see it moving then
In tiny jerks from space to space?
O bright moon rising full and round,
I watch you leave the level ground—
You pass the tops of houses, trees,
I see you mounting over these;
The stars themselves your progress prove—
In vain I watch to see you move—
No single jerk, as yet, I've found!

The Steam Engine

Through the night and through the day
The great steam engine wends his way:
Unswerving, swift, he shall not stray
Though labyrinths of metal thread
Their shining lines before him spread,
And lights are changing green and red!
The great steam-engine tears along,
Of iron and flame, broad-breasted, strong,
His speed is as the eagle's, on
Past startled plain and mountain-height,
This bold embodiment of might
With flame and thunder rends the night!

In the Field

Shade me, pretty buttercup,
Lift your golden goblet up;
I am only a poor spider,
Who has no one else to hide her:
Since my house was swept away
I've been wandering all day!

In the Wood

Said the rabbits to the foxglove,
"Don't you wish that you could scramble
In and out of lofty hedges,
Shady bracken, trailing bramble?
When our play-time is beginning,
And the grasses make long shadows,
Don't you wish that you could join us
Cutting capers in the meadows?"

Jack Frost

Now listen: Once upon a time,
There lived a foolish boy,
Who would not be contented
With any pretty toy.
But one thing he did wish for,
You'll think it very droll—
For sure enough he wanted
To see the great North Pole.
He rode upon a donkey,
Once in the summer weather,
These two fit companions
Went on their way together.
They traveled through great deserts,
And forests that were greater;
They waded through the seas, and then
Jumped over the Equator.
And so they journeyed Northward,
A long, long, weary way;
It was a toilsome journey
for the longest summer day.
At last they reached the great North Pole,
And it, with age, was white;
To see it there so stiff and still
It was a wondrous sight.
Then, foolish boy, he touched it
With one finger—only one—
But quickly he repented
What he had rashly done!

For three tall icebergs round him,
Each shook its great white head,
And then there were no icebergs there,
But three tall men instead.
"Foolish little boy," said one,
"You shall be always cold."
The second said, "And you shall live
Till you are very old."
The third said, "You may tremble,
For all we say is true,
And everything you breathe upon
Shall be as cold as you."
And so it is—we always know
When that little boy is near,
And when our lips are pinched and blue,
We say, "Jack Frost is here."
He walks about at nightfall,
And kills the poor field-mice;
He breathes upon the rivers,
And they are turned to ice.
He passes through our gardens—
We see where he had been,
For every little blade of grass
Is white instead of green;
And if a foolish snowdrop
Lifts up too soon its head,
He holds it in his prickly hand
Till the little thing is dead.
He stays here all the winter,
Sometimes till almost May,
Then come the gentle summer winds
And blow him quite away.

The Moon

There is a lovely lady,
Whom I have often seen,
She's fair and bright and beautiful,
And she was born a queen.
She looks both mild and gentle,
Though she lives in regal state,

And her attendant nobles
In countless myriads wait.
Her mien is humble, and with them
Her dignity she shares,
She would not that her lustrous eye
Should dim the light of theirs.
Upon the ground her beaming smiles
And blessings fall unheard,
She kisses every folded flower
And every silent bird.
If, when we draw our curtains,
We draw them not too tight,
She steals a glance into our room
And wishes us good-night!

My Father Is Extremely Tall

My father is extremely tall
When he stands upright like a wall —
But I am very short and small.
Yet I am growing, so they say,
A little taller every day —
It's not enough to notice it,
Except when dresses will not fit,
And Nurse says, "Let it down a bit."

My Fingers

My ladylike First Finger looks
Extremely grave when up alone —
As though she said, "Now mind your books,
And let your work be nicely done."
My Thumb's a sturdy little chap,
He has no wish to grow up tall,
And says he doesn't care a rap,
Although he's shortest of them all.

The Oak

"Dear me, how nice this rain is," said the Oak,
"I hope at last we're in for a good soak;
My leaves were getting dusty, and my roots
Felt like a tired man's toes inside his boots!"

Pretty Mouse

Pretty mouse, I like to see
Your sparkling eyes look up at me!
Did you leave your home so snug
That I might see you on the rug?
I almost think you came to play
Because I'm not quite well today;
You cannot speak—I'm sure it's true,
And it was very kind of you.
You need not start so, silly mouse,
There's not a cat in all the house!
Besides, you see, I've shut the door,
So you can run all round the floor.
Come hither, and a morsel take
Of this most delicious cake.
You won't—what do you mean to say,
Twisting your nose in that queer way?
You don't believe the cake is nice?
I'm sure it's much too good for mice!
What, you won't taste it! Well, then, don't,
But I shall eat it if you won't.
Ah! Now crumbs are falling fast,
So you've changed your mind at last,
And hither run in scrambling haste,
That you may have a little taste.
But, mouse, I'm quite ashamed to see
You eating crumbs so greedily!
If you go on so fast, you will
Most certainly be very ill.
You've had enough—you're going back
To your small home behind the crack.
Why are you taking that large crumb?
No doubt to give your children some.

Dear mouse—then see—I'll give you more,
Here's a large crumb before your door.
There now—pull harder—pull it through,
And call your friends to feast with you.

The Primrose

The primrose murmured to the wind,
"Drink in my fair scent, and go
And tell the child you left behind,
Where I and hidden violets grow.

"Tell him the squirrels leap the boughs,
The woodpecker goes tap, tap, tap!
While baby rabbits sit and browse
Upon the green turf's mossy lap.

"Tell him that scarlet toadstools stain
The silent pathways through the wood,
The spider weaves a jeweled chain,
The busy ant abroad for food.

"Then bid him" said the primrose, "come
To sing with us, and work and play,
To hear the wild bee's pleasant hum,
And be contented all the day."

The Rainbow

Can that fairy place be found
Where the rainbow touches ground?
Will you tell me, driver, pray,
Is it many miles away?
Somewhere there must be a spot
Shining like a coloured blot,
Pink and purple, blue and green,
Like a transformation scene.
What must all the cattle think
When the grass and flowers turn pink?
Woolly sheep, what do you do
When the daisied field shines blue?

Happy must those children be,
Who the rainbow's end can see,
Who can play and dance and sing
In the rainbow's shining ring!

The Wind

The wind sat idle all day long,
No work to do had he,
He hummed aloud a tuneless song
That passes from tree to tree—
In sighs, sang he.
The wind sat idle till the night,
Then flew by field and town:
The listening children caught no sight
Of fleeting beard, or brown
And windy gown.

The Raindrops

Some raindrops hung from a bar,
And they couldn't tell when to drop;
"The ground," said one, "is so far,
That I'm rather inclined to stop."
"Oh," sighed another, "the art
Consists in getting much rounder."
"I'm off!" cried one, with a start
Of blank amazement and wonder.

Responsibility

Each thought I think, each little word I say,
Goes traveling outwards far and far away,
And like a bottle drifting on the sea,
None know where its landing-place will be.

River, River

River, river, running through the land,
Are you a traveler over foreign sand?
Are you a carrier from town to town,
River, river, as you hurry down?

Yes, I'm a carrier from town to town:
Here are ships with white sails, there are boats with brown,
What shall they bring you, what will you send?
I'll be your carrier to the land's end.

The Sailor

The sailor comes from over seas,
From lands where we have never been,
Where flowers are strange, and strange the trees—
Such golden fruit amongst the green!
The birds wear rainbows in their wings,
What fire and flash, what shine and sheen,
They seem too fine for mortal things!
Gay are the songs the sailor sings
When home he comes from over seas.

The Shepherd Boy

The farmer's shepherd boy is Bill:
Across the fields he drives the sheep,
And where the long road winds uphill,
Like little summer clouds they creep.
And Bill is like the gentle wind,
He whistles softly as he goes,
He calls them where he had a mind,
And never uses threats or blows.

The Snow Queen

Where the wild bear clasps the ice
Over the hanging precipice,
Where the glittering icebergs shine
Within the sunset, red as wine,
Where the reindeer lick the snow,
To see what there may be below,
Where the shades are blue and green,
There lives, they say, the great Snow Queen.
Wild her eyes are as the sea
When northern winds blow lustily.

Her queenly robes are white as snow,
But flaming diamonds on them glow,
And many a precious stone.
Of green ice builded is her throne:
Polar bears her watch-dogs are—
Her only lamp, an evening star.

Swinging

Swing me up and swing me down,
Swing me up towards the sky —
Swinging is like being blown,
Blow me up and let me fly,
Like a piece of thistledown —
Swing me up towards the sky!

The Windmill

"I'm busy now," the windmill said,
Waving his arms about his head;
"Don't interrupt me while I'm grinding
The flour to make the baker's bread."

To a Bee

Busy Bee, busy Bee, where are you going?
Down where the bluebells are budding blowing,
There I shall find something hidden and sweet
That all little children are willing to eat!
Busy Bee, busy Bee, what will you do?
Put it into my pocket, and save it for you!

When the Great Wind

When the great wind goes panting round the world,
Licking the seas, and sniffing through the lands,
I, in my bed, am lying closely curled,
Thinking of all that no one understands,
When the great wind goes panting round the world!

Who Blows You Out?

O little round and yellow moon,
Why have you lit yourself so soon?
Jane won't bring in the lamp for me,
She says it's light enough to see!
Perhaps you did not know the time,
But don't you hear the church clock chime?
Who blows you out, I wonder, when
The shining day comes back again?

Who Is That Singing?

Who is that singing up in the chimney?
Who is that whistling through the bare trees?
That is the wind who flies as he listeth,
That is the wind whom nobody sees.

Wildflowers

Yellow Kingcup, is it true
That Fairie Kings drink out of you,
Golden Kingcup full of dew?
"My cup is filled," the flower replies,
"For Kings and Queens and butterflies."
Creeping scarlet Pimpernel,
With your closed or opened bell,
Do you shower and shine foretell?
"Low lying on the dusty grass,
I am the poor man's weather-glass."
Fiery Golans, you who glow
Like suns upon the marshes low,
From Earth or heaven do you grow?
"A giant dropped us from his car,
Flakes of the sun's own fire we are."
Daisy, with a yellow breast,
More beautiful than all the rest,
'Tis you can say who loves us best.
"I rise and spread beneath your feet,
In silver leaves, my portents sweet."

Wishes

O give me the ears of a fairy
To hear the trees growing,
The greeting of ants and of earwigs;
To hearken the lowing
Of tiny green cattle in grass woods
Where wee winds are blowing.
O give me ears of a giant
To hear the sun thunder
Along space, to list the moon coming,
the earth swinging under:
Ah! we hear not and see not, but thinking
Fills life up with wonder.

Poems by Edward Lear

(from *A Book of Nonsense*)

Edward Lear was a master of the limerick, a form of poetry that often includes a funny twist. These are fun to recite because of their catchy rhyme scheme (AABBA) and the rollicking rhythm.

There was a Young Lady whose bonnet,
Came untied when the birds sat upon it;
But she said: "I don't care!
All the birds in the air
Are welcome to sit on my bonnet!"

There was an Old Lady of Chertsey,
Who made a remarkable curtsey;
She twirled round and round,
Till she sunk underground,
Which distressed all the people of Chertsey.

There was an Old Man in a tree,
Who was horribly bored by a Bee;
When they said, "Does it buzz?"
He replied, "Yes, it does!
"It's a regular brute of a Bee!"

There was an Old Man who supposed,
That the street door was partially closed;
But some very large rats,
Ate his coats and his hats,
While that futile old gentleman dozed.

There was a Young Lady whose eyes,
Were unique as to color and size
When she opened them wide,
People all turned aside,
And started away in surprise.

There was a Young Lady of Dorking,
Who bought a large bonnet for walking;
But its colour and size
So bedazzled her eyes,
That she very soon went back to Dorking.

There was an Old Man with a beard,
Who said, "It is just as I feared!
"Two Owls and a Hen,
Four Larks and a Wren,
"Have all built their nests in my beard!"

There was an Old Man of the West,
Who wore a pale plum-colored vest;
When they said, "Does it fit?"
He replied, "Not a bit!"
That uneasy Old Man of the West.

There was an Old Man of the Isles,
Whose face was pervaded with smiles;
He sung high dum diddle,
And played on the fiddle,
That amiable Man of the Isles.

There was a Young Lady whose chin,
Resembled the point of a pin;
So she had it made sharp,
And purchased a harp,
And played several tunes with her chin.

There was an Old Man of Kilkenny,
Who never had more than a penny;
He spent all that money,
In onion and honey,
That wayward Old Man of Kilkenny.

There was a Young Lady of Portugal,
Whose ideas were excessively nautical:
She climbed up a tree,
To examine the sea,
But declared she would never leave Portugal.

There was an Old Person of Leeds,
Whose head was infested with beads;
She sat on a stool,
And ate gooseberry fool,
Which agreed with that person of Leeds.

There was a Young Lady of Norway,
Who casually sat on a doorway;
When the door squeezed her flat,
She exclaimed, 'What of that?'
This courageous Young Lady of Norway.

There was an Old Person whose habits,
Induced him to feed upon rabbits;
When he'd eaten eighteen,
He turned perfectly green,
Upon which he relinquished those habits.

There was an Old Person of Dover,
Who rushed through a field of blue Clover;
But some very large bees
Stung his nose and his knees,
So he very soon went back to Dover.

There was an Old Person of Basing,
Whose presence of mind was amazing;
He purchased a steed,
Which he rode at full speed,
And escaped from the people of Basing.

There was an Old Man of the Wrekin
Whose shoes made a horrible creaking
But they said, 'Tell us whether
Your shoes are of leather,
Or of what, you Old Man of the Wrekin?'

There was a Young Lady of Bute,
Who played on a silver-gilt flute;
She played several jigs,
To her uncle's white pigs,
That amusing Young Lady of Bute.

There was an Old Person of Rhodes,
Who strongly objected to toads;
He paid several cousins
To catch them by dozens,
That futile Old Person of Rhodes.

There was a Young Lady of Ryde,
Whose shoe-strings were seldom untied.
She purchased some clogs,
And some small spotted dogs,
And frequently walked about Ryde.

There was an Old Man with a nose,
Who said, 'If you choose to suppose,
That my nose is too long,
You are certainly wrong!'
That remarkable Man with a nose.

There was an Old Man on a hill,
Who seldom, if ever, stood still;
He ran up and down,
In his Grandmother's gown,
Which adorned that Old Man on a hill.

There was an Old Person of Chili,
Whose conduct was painful and silly,
He sat on the stairs,
Eating apples and pears,
That imprudent Old Person of Chili.

Poems by Dollie Radford

(from *The Young Gardeners' Kalendar*)

January

Trees look empty, branches bare,
When the busy months begin,
Gardeners all must have a care
Not to stay too much within.
Catkins, on the hazel, show
Garden work has well begun;
Snowdrops in the shining row
Blossom in the winter sun.
Brush the Old Year leaves away,
Make the New Year garden neat,
Gardeners must not stop for play
Till their labor is complete.

February

Of all sweet days that come and go,
The sweetest fall
When first the almond blossoms show,
Above the wall:
When through their flowers a cloudless sky
shines clear and blue,
You know the spring will soon be by
with flowers for you.
Then sow your treasured seeds nor let
the month grow old,
Ere borage and sweet thyme are set,
And marigold:
Put larkspurs, too, beside the gate
Among the grass,
Like sentinels in blue, to wait
when friends do pass;
And sweet-peas in a gracious line,
To make a blaze
Of rainbow colours, rich and fine,
In summer days.

March

Purple, white and yellow cup,
Now the crocus reaches up
Treasured blossoms, every one,
Fearless to the wind and sun.
Hyacinths with stately heads,
Make processions through the beds,
while the little squills dance by
In the color of the sky.
Now beside the privet row,
Many dainty windflowers blow,
Strayed sweet dwellers of the wood,
Come to stay with you for good.
You must then sow speedily,
Hollyhocks and honesty,
Gilliflowers and columbine,
Sweetly scented eglantine—
Canterbury bells, to ring
Summer in the triumphing,
And nasturtiums bright, to fill
Every empty windowsill.
Little slips of lavender—
Where no busy feet do stir,
Southernwood for bushes high,
Rosemary for by and by—
Plant them all while March is here:
While his crest and flashing spear
Shine throughout the happy land,
Do your work with joyous hands.

April

Through the meadow April comes,
Leaving, as he passes,
Companies of daffodils
All among the grasses.
Tulips round about the door,
Ranged in martial order;
Violets in sweet array,
Up and down the border.
And beside the lily-pond,
Mindful of its sleepers,
Guards of light frittillaries,
For its fairy keepers.
Sow your fine chrysanthemums
While he blithely passes,
Dahlias too, and thrift, to blow
All among your grasses.

May

Red may and white may shine
All round the lawn,
Lilac and goldenrain
Show there at dawn:
There the big chestnuts stand
In a great row,
Mountains where fairies build
Castles of snow:
Down all the grassy slopes
Cowslips are gay,
Green banks are yellow where
Primroses stray.
Pear-bloom and plum now lie
Thick on the trees,
Cherry with lighter hold
Stirs in the breeze.
Now from their leafy beds
Lilies do bring

Rarest of all the rare
Perfumes of Spring.
Set all your seedlings out,
May sun is strong,
Through all the garden beds
Spread them along.
Carefully weed, and then
Sow Mignonette,
Pinks and sweet-williams ere
May month has set.

June

Roses pink and roses red,
Hold a court in every bed;
Stately lilies tall and white,
Pay them homage day and night.
Marigolds and poppies show
In a rich and radiant row,
And beyond their splendid line,
Irises in purple shine.
Honeysuckle scents the air,
Loveliness is everywhere,
And beside the border-grass
Venus's own looking-glass.
Now the privet bears its flowers,
Now the petals fall in showers
Where a white syringe-tree
Guards the homely honest.
Bulbs must come from out the ground,
Young ones must be good and sound,
And with care be put away
For another gardening day.
Water well, and tie, and trim,
June fills quickly to the brim,
Fills with work for those who'd be
Helpers in her husbandry.

July

Jasmine blossoms round the arbor,
Elder spreads along the air,
Hollyhocks stand proudly tallest
In the fragrant thoroughfare.
Pansies, like a 'broidered carpet,
Through the garden ways are set,
And the sweet-peas catch the sunlight
In a tangled flowery net.
Sunflowers, with a kingly bearing,
Hold their golden heads on high,
Pinks breathe out a friendly welcome
Every time you pass them by.
Gather seeds while seeds do ripen
In the bounteous July sun,
Garner well the treasure-packets
In your storehouse one by one.
And before the month is over,
Pluck sweet lavender and dry
All its tiny flowers for sweetness,
In the winter by and by.

August

Like a delicate sea coral,
Barberry shines here and there,
Through the brightness of a garden
Filled with all the summer's ware;
And the fuchsia hangs its blossom
In the richly scented air.
Passionflowers in sober beauty,
Through the trellis twine and twist,
And the stocks breathe out their fragrance
Near the sweet love-in-a-mist;
Where the bees all day for gladness
In their honey-search persist.
Cut your box and mow your grass now,
Lest they grow too thin and high,
Gather herbs too, for distilling,

As was done in days gone by,
For the old ways are the wisest
When our gardening plans run high.

September

September brings the ripening sun,
The clear sharp morning air,
And asters in a border wide,
And daisies for the garden's pride,
And foxgloves everywhere.
Among the rushes and the reeds
Long purples bend and sway,
Between the water and the land,
Beside the shining stream they stand
Till Autumn fades away.
Plant crocuses and tulips rare,
To bloom in next Year's Spring,
And crown imperials rich and fine,
To stand up in a glorious line
Amid new blossoming.

October

Where the beech and maple grow
Leaves as bright as flowers show,
Every path, and garden bed,
Are ablaze with gold and red.
Down the lane, and through the stiles,
Berries shine for miles and miles,
Hips and haws and nightshade deep,
Do the hedge-rows festal keep.
For your happy wearing see,
Matchless wreaths of briony,
Fairer than a jeweled crown
For a child to gather down.
Now is pleasant work all-day,
In the orchard where you play,
Laden branches bid you sing
Of a plenteous gathering.

November

Still the garden blossoms bravely,
Though the Year is nearly done,
Fresh chrysanthemums are shining
In the pale and wintry sun.
Such a number of bright colors
Make the beds and borders plain,
We believe the summer roses
Must have all come back again.
Now's the time when great plantations
Must be planted, oak and fir,
Beech and elm, and towering poplar
That the wandering night-winds stir.
And the time when treasured fruit-stones,
In the summer stored away,
Must be set, that spreading orchards
May grow up another day.

December

No gardener need go far to find
The Christmas rose,
The fairest of the flowers that mark
The sweet year's close:
Nor be in quest of places where
The hollies grow,
Nor seek for sacred trees that hold
The mistletoe.
All kingly tended gardens love
December days,
And spread their latest riches out
In winter's praise.
But every gardener's work this month
Must surely be
To choose a very beautiful
Big Christmas tree,
And see it through the open door
In triumph ride,
To reign a glorious reign within
At Christmas-tide.

Poems by Robert Louis Stevenson

(from *A Child's Garden of Verses*)

At the Sea Side

When I was down beside the sea
A wooden spade they gave to me
   To dig the sandy shore.
My hole were empty like a cup.
In every hole the sea came up,
   Till it could come no more.

Bed in Summer

In winter I get up at night
And dress by yellow candle-light.
In summer quite the other way,
I have to go to bed by day.

I have to go to bed and see
The birds still hopping on the tree,
Or hear the grown-up people's feet
Still going past me in the street.

And does it not seem hard to you,
When all the sky is clear and blue,
And I should like so much to play,
To have to go to bed by day?

Block City

What are you able to build with your blocks?
Castles and palaces, temples and docks.
Rain may keep raining, and others go roam,
But I can be happy and building at home.

Let the sofa be mountains, the carpet be sea,
There I'll establish a city for me:
A kirk and a mill and a palace beside,
And a harbor as well where my vessels may ride.

Great is the palace with pillar and wall,
A sort of a tower on the top of it all,
And steps coming down in an orderly way
To where my toy vessels lie safe in the bay.

This one is sailing and that one is moored:
Hark to the song of the sailors on board!
And see, on the steps of my palace, the kings
Coming and going with presents and things!

Now I have done with it, down let it go!
And all in a moment the town is laid low.
Block upon block lying scattered and free,
What is there left of my town by the sea?

Yet as I saw it, I see it again,
The kirk and the palace, the ships and the men,
And as long as I live and where'er I may be,
I'll always remember my town by the sea.

The Cow

The friendly cow all red and white,
　　I love with all my heart:
She gives me cream with all her might,
　　To eat with apple-tart.

She wanders lowing here and there,
　　And yet she cannot stray,
All in the pleasant open air,
　　The pleasant light of day;

And blown by all the winds that pass
　　And wet with all the showers,
She walks among the meadow grass
　　And eats the meadow flowers.

Fairy Bread

Come up here, O dusty feet!
    Here is fairy bread to eat.
Here in my retiring room,
Children, you may dine
On the golden smell of broom
    And the shade of pine;
And when you have eaten well,
Fairy stories hear and tell.

The Flowers

All the names I know from nurse:
Gardener's garters, Shepherd's purse,
Bachelor's buttons, Lady's smock,
And the Lady Hollyhock.

Fairy places, fairy things,
Fairy woods where the wild bee wings,
Tiny trees for tiny dames—
These must all be fairy names!

Tiny woods below whose boughs
shady fairies weave a house;
Tiny treetops, rose or thyme,
Where the braver fairies climb!

Fair are grown-up people's trees,
But the fairest woods are these;
Where, if I were not so tall,
I should live for good and all.

Foreign Lands

Up into the cherry tree
Who should climb but little me?
I held the trunk with both my hands
And looked abroad in foreign lands.

I saw the next door garden lie,
Adorned with flowers, before my eye,
And many pleasant places more
That I had never seen before.

I saw the dimpling river pass
And be the sky's blue looking-glass;
The dusty roads go up and down
With people tramping in to town.

If I could find a higher tree
Farther and farther I should see,
To where the grown-up river slips
Into the sea among the ships,

To where the roads on either hand
Lead onward into fairy land,
Where all the children dine at five,
And all the playthings come alive.

Happy Thoughts

The world is so full of a number of things,
I'm sure we should all be as happy as kings.

The Land of Nod

From breakfast on through all the day
At home among my friends I stay,
But every night I go abroad
Afar into the Land of Nod.

All by myself I have to go,
With none to tell me what to do—
All alone beside the streams
And up the mountain-sides of dreams.

The strangest things are these for me,
Both things to eat and things to see,
And many frightening sights abroad
Till morning in the Land of Nod.

Try as I like to find the way,
I never can get back by day,
Nor can remember plain and clear
The curious music that I hear.

The Little Land

When at home alone I sit
And am very tired of it,
I have just to shut my eyes
To go sailing through the skies—
To go sailing far away
To the pleasant Land of Play;
To the fairy land afar
Where the Little People are;
Where the clover-tops are trees,
And the rain-pools are the seas,
And the leaves, like little ships,
Sail about on tiny trips;
And above the daisy tree
    Through the grasses,
High o'erhead the Bumble Bee
    Hums and passes.

In the forest to and fro
I can wander, I can go;
See the spider and the fly,
And the ants go marching by,
Carrying parcels with their feet
Down the green and grassy street.
I can in the sorrel sit

Where the ladybird alit.
I can climb the jointed grass
   And on high
See the greater swallows pass
   In the sky,
And the round sun rolling by
Heeding no such things as I.

Through that forest I can pass
Till, as in a looking-glass,
Humming fly and daisy tree
And my tiny self I see,
Painted very clear and neat
On the rain-pool at my feet.
Should a leaflet come to land
Drifting near to where I stand,
Straight I'll board that tiny boat
Round the rain-pool sea to float.

Little thoughtful creatures sit
On the grassy coasts of it;
Little things with lovely eyes
See me sailing with surprise.
Some are clad in armour green—
(These have sure to battle been!)—
Some are pied with ev'ry hue,
Black and crimson, gold and blue;
Some have wings and swift are gone—
But they all look kindly on.

When my eyes I once again
Open, and see all things plain:
High bare walls, great bare floor;
Great big knobs on drawer and door;
Great big people perched on chairs,
Stitching tucks and mending tears,
Each a hill that I could climb,
And talking nonsense all the time—
   O dear me,
   That I could be

A sailor on the rain-pool sea,
A climber in the clover tree,
And just come back a sleepy-head,
Late at night to go to bed.

My Kingdom

Down by a shining water well
I found a very little dell,
    No higher than my head.
The heather and the gorse about
In summer bloom were coming out,
    Some yellow and some red.

I called the little pool a sea;
The little hills were big to me;
    For I am very small.
I made a boat, I made a town,
I searched the caverns up and down,
    And named them one and all.

And all about was mine, I said,
The little sparrows overhead,
    The little minnows too.
This was the world and I was king;
For me the bees came by to sing,
    For me the swallow flew.

I played there were no deeper seas,
Nor any wider plains than these,
    Nor other kings than me.
At last I heard my mother call
Out from the house at evenfall,
    To call me home to tea.

And I must rise and leave my dell,
And leave my dimpled water well,
    And leave my heather blooms.
Alas! and as my home I neared,
How very big my nurse appeared.
    How great and cool the rooms!

My Shadow

I have a little shadow that goes in and out with me,
And what can be the use of him is more than I can see.
His is very, very like me from the heels up to the head;
And I see him jump before me, when I jump into my bed.

The funniest thing about him is the way he likes to grow—
Not at all like proper children, which is always very slow;
For he sometimes shoots up taller like an India-rubber ball,
And he sometimes goes so little that there's none of him at all.

He hasn't got a notion of how children ought to play,
And can only make a fool of me in every sort of way.
He stays so close behind me, he's a coward you can see;
I'd think shame to stick to nursie as that shadow sticks to me!

One morning, very early, before the sun was up,
I rose and found the shining dew on every buttercup;
But my lazy little shadow, like an arrant sleepy-head,
Had stayed at home behind me and was fast asleep in bed.

Nest Eggs

Birds all the summer day
    Flutter and quarrel
Here in the arbor-like
    Tent of the laurel.

Here in the fork
    The brown nest is seated;
Four little blue eggs
    The mother keeps heated.

While we stand watching her
    Staring like gabies,
Safe in each egg are the
    Bird's little babies

Soon the frail eggs they shall
    Chip, and upspringing

Make all the April woods
    Merry with singing.

Younger than we are,
    O children, and frailer,
Soon in the blue air they'll be,
    Singer and sailor.

We, so much older,
    Taller and stronger,
We shall look down on the
    Birdies no longer.

They shall go flying
    With musical speeches
High overhead in the
    Tops of the beeches.

In spite of our wisdom
    And sensible talking,
We on our feet must go
    Plodding and walking.

Rain

The rain is falling all around,
    It falls on field and tree,
It rains on the umbrellas here,
    And on the ships at sea.

Singing

Of speckled eggs the birdie sings
    And nests among the trees;
The sailor sings of ropes and things
    In ships upon the seas.

The children sing in far Japan,
    The children sing in Spain;
The organ with the organ man
    Is singing in the rain.

The Sun's Travels

The sun is not a-bed, when I
At night upon my pillow lie;
Still round the Earth his way he takes,
And morning after morning makes.

While here at home, in shining day,
We round the sunny garden play,
Each little Indian sleepy-head
Is being kissed and put to bed.

And when at eve I rise from tea,
Day dawns beyond the Atlantic Sea;
And all the children in the west
Are getting up and being dressed.

The Swing

How do you like to go up in a swing,
    Up in the air so blue?
Oh, I do think it the pleasantest thing
    Ever a child can do!

Up in the air and over the wall,
    Till I can see so wide,
River and trees and cattle and all
    Over the countryside —

Till I look down on the garden green,
    Down on the roof so brown —
Up in the air I go flying again,
    Up in the air and down!

Time to Rise

A birdie with a yellow bill
Hopped upon my window sill,
Cocked his shining eye and said:
"Ain't you 'shamed, you sleepy-head!"

To Any Reader

As from the house your mother sees
You playing round the garden trees,
So you may see, if you will look
Through the windows of this book,
Another child, far, far away,
And in another garden, play.
But do not think you can at all,
By knocking on the window, call
That child to hear you. He intent
Is all on his play-business bent.
He does not hear; he will not look,
Nor yet be lured out of this book.
For, long ago, the truth to say,
He had grown up and gone away,
And it is but a child of air
That lingers in the garden there.

Where Go the Boats?

Dark brown is the river,
    Golden is the sand.
It flows along for ever,
    With trees on either hand.

Green leaves a-floating,
    Castles of the foam,
Boats of mine a-boating—
    Where will all come home?

On goes the river
    And out past the mill,
Away down the valley,
    Away down the hill.

Away down the river,
    A hundred miles or more,
Other little children
    Shall bring my boats ashore.

The Wind

I saw you toss the kites on high
And blow the birds about the sky;
And all around I heard you pass,
Like ladies' skirts across the grass—
    O wind, a-blowing all day long,
    O wind, that sings so loud a song!

I saw the different things you did,
But always you yourself you hid.
I felt you push, I heard you call,
I could not see yourself at all—
    O wind, a-blowing all day long,
    O wind, that sings so loud a song!

O you that are so strong and cold,
O blower, are you young or old?
Are you a beast of field and tree,
Or just a stronger child than me?
    O wind, a-blowing all day long,
    O wind, that sings so loud a song!

Windy Nights

Whenever the moon and stars are set,
    Whenever the wind is high,
All night long in the dark and wet,
    A man goes riding by.
Late in the night when the fires are out,
Why does he gallop and gallop about?

Whenever the trees are crying aloud,
    And ships are tossed at sea,
By, on the highway, low and loud,
    By at the gallop goes he.
By at the gallop he goes, and then
By he comes back at the gallop again.

Verses and Poems Especially for Grade 3

Am I

(Add gestures to indicate "above" and "below.")

Upon the Earth I stand upright.
I lift my arms up to the light.
My feet Earth-bound below remain.
Hands and feet together again.
Hands above . . . feet below . . .
Here in the middle am I!

Autumn Color

(This is a nice descriptive verse of Lady Autumn. Movement with silks may be fun here. If it is warm outside, play in the leaves with autumn verses!)

The world is full of color! 'Tis autumn once again,
And leaves of gold and crimson, are lying in the lane.
There are brown and yellow acorns, berries and hips of rose,
Golden broom and purple heather growing near the road.
Green apples in the orchard, flushed by the growing sun;
Mellow pears and brambles when the colored pheasants run!
Yellow, blue, and orange, russet, rose and red;
A gaily colored pageant, an autumn flower bed.

Building a House

(You can add house building gestures or even build as you go!)

Let us bravely now build with fine bricks both a high and handsome house.
That it first may be firm and well founded, we will dig a good depth for foundations.
On the clay we will cast molds of concrete, then we'll mix and we'll make good mortar.

The bricks layer upon layer we will lay, till the top is as tall as the trees.

As it grows we leave gaps for some glass, that the sunlight in splendor may stream.

It has views over vale and over valley, with its polish and paint it looks proud.

And we know we have nothing neglected.

Cow Talk

(This is a funny, rambling poem, moseying along just as a cow might! It paints an amusing picture of two cows with nothing much to do. The children really enjoy living into the cow's slow, ponderous nature.)

Half the time they munched the grass

And all the time they lay

Down in the water-meadows,

in the lazy month of May.

A-chewing and a-mooing

To pass the hours away.

"Nice weather," said the brown cow.

"Ah," said the white.

"Grass is very tasty,"

"Grass is all right."

Half the time they munched the grass

And all the time they lay

Down in the water-meadows,

in the lazy month of May.

A-chewing and a-mooing,

To pass the hours away.

"Rain coming," said the brown cow.

"Ah," said the white.

"Flies are very tiresome."

"Flies bite."

Farewell Summer

(This is a fun verse to act out. If you have many family members participating, you can take turns being various animals with a narrator.)

The maples flare among the spruces,
The bursting foxgrape spills its juices;
The gentians lift their sapphire fringes,
On roadways rich with golden tinges.
The waddling woodchucks fill their hampers,
The deermouse runs, the chipmunk scampers.
The squirrels scurry, never stopping,
For all they hear is apples dropping.
With walnuts plumping fast and faster,
The bees weigh down the purple aster.
Yes, hive your honey, little hummer,
The woods are waving, "Farewell summer."

The Farmer

(This verse can be performed through movement or recited and memorized as speech work.)

To dig the ditch,
To plough the land,
To this the farmer
Turns a hand.
To sow the seed,
To hoe and weed,
To give the plants
The light they need.
To milk the cows,
To feed the hens,
To clean the pigs
Within their pens.
To cut the corn,
To store the grain,
To bring the sheep
To be sheared again.
To care for the soil,

To let it rest,
To feed it—so
It gives its best.
The farmer works
And so do we,
Helping flower,
Bird, and bee.

Go with Me

(Repeat a minimum of three times. Speak faster and faster, as fast as you can.)

Though they go there with me,
I will go there with thee,
Then we'll all go together.
How funny that will be!
For these are these and those are those,
As soon as we come hither.
But these are those and those are these
As soon as we go thither.

In March

(This verse can be used as a challenge for poetry memorization or it can be performed as role play. It is fun to act like a storm!)

In March the wind blows loud and strong
And roars among the trees.
It sings a wild exultant song
Like waves on stormy seas.
The tossing branches madly strive,
The treetops bow before its drive.
Assaulted by the frantic gale,
The slender branches yield.
It seems their strength cannot prevail
On such a battlefield.
Yet when the wind is dead and gone
Unharmed the frail young buds live on.

Jangling Jam Jars

Jangling our jam jars and jumping for joy,
Far from the village a journey we make.
Ranging the generous hedges and fields,
Juicy jet blackberries gently to take.

Mighty Smith

(This is a powerful verse for children of this age. It truly speaks to their need for skill and strength! You can act it out, varying the strength of your tone and motion with the verse.)

Cling! Cling! Clang! Ring! Ting! Cling! Hark to the blow of the hammer.
High overhead it is held. Down it drives, down into the darkness.
Shaping the steel with its spell.
Blow bellows blow, down below, glow red coals, glow hot and slow,
Flash and fly! Sparks on high, gleam and die.
Cold and dark, stiff and stark, lies the iron.
Thrust it into the heart of the fire. Cherry red first it grows
Then to orange it glows, till it burns with the brightest of light.
Pull it out! Beat and pound! Hammer heard all around!
Ring! Ting! Cling! Hear the anvil's sound.
Mighty smith bend and twist, ne'er a stroke have you missed,
See the horseshoe is fashioned all round.
With your tongs hold it fast, into the water at last,
The horseshoe must plunge to be hardened.
Zish, swish, sputter, splish! The iron cools and is darkened
With your hands hold it fast . . . finished at last!

My Heart

(This is a lovely morning verse. The gestures here should indicate the inner light and its ability to extend outwardly.)

I am strong, I am brave, I am valiant and bold.
For the sun fills my heart with its life giving gold.
I am helpful and truthful and loving and free.
For my heart's inner sunshine glows brightly in me.
I will open my heart to the sunbeams so bright;
I will warm all the world with my heart's inner light.

November Comes

November comes, and November goes,
With the last red berries and the first white snows.
With night coming early and dawn coming late,
And ice in the bucket and frost by the gate.
The fires burn and kettles sing,
And Earth sinks to rest
Until next spring.

The Pasture

by Robert Frost

I'm going out to clean the pasture spring;
I'll only stop to rake the leaves away
(And wait to watch the water clear, I may):
I sha'n't be gone long—You come too.

I'm going out to fetch the little calf
That's standing by the mother. It's so young,
It totters when she licks it with her tongue.
I sha'n't be gone long—You come too.

Punctuation Matters

(Children retain information best if there is a clear picture behind it. Giving the punctuation marks life allows children to integrate them more fully.)

I am the period, I love to rest.
All sentences stop at my request.
I want to know, what is your name?
Where do you live? What is your fame?
The question mark, oh yes, am I,
So what is the answer? Can you tell me why?
Whoopee! Hooray! Look out! Make way!
I'm here! I'm there! I'm everywhere!
Whatever the excitement rare,
the exclamation point is there!

Seeing Ghosts

Amidst the mists and coldest frosts,
With barest wrists and stoutest boasts,
He thrust his fists against the posts
And still insists he sees the ghosts.

Stopping by Woods on a Snowy Evening

by Robert Frost

Whose woods these are I think I know.
His house is in the village, though;
He will not see me stopping here
To watch his woods fill up with snow.

My little horse must think it queer
To stop without a farmhouse near
Between the woods and frozen lake
The darkest evening of the year.

He gives his harness bells a shake
To ask if there is some mistake.
The only other sound's the sweep
Of easy wind and downy flake.

The woods are lovely, dark and deep,
But I have promises to keep,
And miles to go before I sleep,
And miles to go before I sleep.

Sugar Camp

(This verse, based on a Chippewa melody, describes the Chippewa tribe's method for making maple syrup in the spring. It can be chanted with a strong rhythm. Add gestures to describe the activity. This is particularly nice when followed by maple candy!)

Let us go to the sugar camp while the snow lies on the ground.
Live in the birch-bark wigwam, all the children and the older folk
While the people are at work.
Cut a notch in the maple tree, set a pail on the ground below.
Soon the sap will be flowing, from the tree it will be flowing.
All the people are at work.

Make a fire in the sugar lodge so that we may boil the sap.
Soon the sap will be flowing, from the tree it will be flowing.
All the people are at work.
In the snow see the rabbit tracks, hear the note of the chick-a-dee.
We must not stop to follow them, 'tis the season of the sugar camp.
All the people are at work.
Bring the sap from the maple trees, pour the sap in the iron pot.
See how it steams and bubbles. May we have a taste of it?
All the people are at work.
Pour the syrup in the graining trough. Stir it slowly as it thicker grows.
Now it has changed to sugar. We may eat it in the birchbark dish.
There is sugar for us all.

Two Hands We Have

(This poem meets third graders in their need to feel competent with practical tasks. This can be memorized and used as a movement exercise. It can also be used to practice recognizing parts of speech, such as clap for the nouns, stomp for the adjectives, and jump for the verbs.)

Two hands we have with fingers four,
How hard it would be if there were more.
And yet we need them all with the thumb, too,
To do all the things that we want to do.
We can paint and clench and shake and mold,
We can press and lift and stroke and hold,
We can push and pull and wave and beckon,
With both hands we can even reckon!
When we have tools we can do much more,
With a spade we dig, with a drill we bore,
With a knife we cut, with a fork we eat,
With a spoon we stir, or our bread we beat.
With two needles we knit, with one we sew,
If it has an eye in which the thread will go.
With a crayon we draw, with a brush we paint,
Our colors can either be strong or faint.
All these things we alone can do,
For of legs and feet we have only two.
And our hands and arms we carry free
The world and our fellows to serve worthily.

The Village Blacksmith

by Henry Wadsworth Longfellow

Under a spreading chestnut-tree
    The village smithy stands;
The smith, a mighty man is he,
    With large and sinewy hands;
And the muscles of his brawny arms
    Are strong as iron bands.

His hair is crisp, and black, and long,
    His face is like the tan;
His brow is wet with honest sweat,
    He earns whate'er he can,
And looks the whole world in the face,
    For he owes not any man.

Week in, week out, from morn till night,
    You can hear his bellows blow;
You can hear him swing his heavy sledge,
    With measured beat and slow,
Like a sexton ringing the village bell,
    When the evening sun is low.

And children coming home from school
    Look in at the open door;
They love to see the flaming forge,
    And hear the bellows roar,
And catch the burning sparks that fly
    Like chaff from threshing-floor.

Toiling—rejoicing—sorrowing,
    Onward through life he goes;
Each morning sees some task begin,
    Each evening sees it close;
Something attempted, something done,
    Has earned a night's repose.

Thanks, thanks to thee, my worthy friend,
　For the lesson thou hast taught!
Thus at the flaming forge of life
　Our fortunes must be wrought;
Thus on its sounding anvil shaped
　Each burning deed and thought.

We Do

(This verse is quite grounding and holds a strong rhythm for movement as well as clapping exercises.)

The Farmer is sowing the seed,
In the field he is sowing the seed.
The Reaper is cutting the hay,
In the meadow he is cutting the hay.
The Gardener is digging the ground,
In the garden he is digging the ground.
The Woodsman is chopping the tree,
In the forest he is chopping the tree.
The Fisher is drawing the nets,
In the sea he is drawing the nets.
The Builder is laying the bricks,
In the wall he is laying the bricks.
The Cobbler is mending the shoes,
In the shop he is mending the shoes.
The Miller is grinding the corn,
In the mill he is grinding the corn.
The Baker is kneading the dough,
In the kitchen he is kneading the dough.

When I Wake

(This lovely verse speaks both to the third grader's new sense of being separate from the world as well as affirming the child's need for connection. The imagery provides a background for gestures that reflect the interconnectedness of life.)

When I wake in the early mist
The sun has hardly shown,
And everything is still asleep
And I'm awake alone.
The stars are faint and flickering.
The sun is new and shy.

All the world sleeps quietly,
Except the sun and I.
And then beginning noises start,
The whirrs and huffs and hums,
The birds peep out to find a worm,
The mice squeak out for crumbs.
The calf moos out to find the cow,
And taste the morning air
And everything is awake
And running everywhere.
The dew has dried,
The fields are warm,
The day is loud and bright,
And I'm the one who woke the sun
And kissed the stars good-night.

Winken, Blinken, and Nod

by Eugene Field

Winken, Blinken, and Nod one night
    Sailed off in a wooden shoe—
Sailed off on a river of crystal light,
    Into a sea of dew.
"Where are you going, and what do you wish?"
    The old moon asked the three.
"We have come to fish for the herring fish
    That live in the beautiful sea;
    Nets of silver and gold have we!"
            Said Winken,
            Blinken,
            And Nod.

The old moon laughed and sang a song,
    As they rocked in the wooden shoe,
And the wind that sped them all night long
    Ruffled the waves of dew.
The little stars were the herring fish
    That lived in the beautiful sea—
"Now cast your nets wherever you wish—
    Never afeared are we;"

So cried the stars to the fisherman three:
> Winken,

> Blinken,

> And Nod.

All night long their nets they threw
> To the stars in the twinkling foam—

Then down from the skies came the wooden shoe
> Bringing the fishermen home;

'Twas all so pretty a sail it seemed
> As if it could not be,

And some folks thought 'twas a dream they'd dreamed
> Of sailing that beautiful sea—

> But I shall name you the fishermen three:

>> Winken,

>> Blinken,

>> And Nod.

Wynken and Blynken are two little eyes,
> And Nod is a little head,

And the wooden shoe that sailed the skies
> Is a wee one's trundle-bed;

So shut your eyes while Mother sings
> Of wonderful sights that be,

And you shall see the beautiful things
> As you rock in the misty sea

> Where the old shoe rocked the fishermen three:—

>> Wynken,

>> Blynken,

>> And Nod.

List of Songs, Verses, Fingerplays, and Poems

Verses in Alphabetical Order

A Diller, a Dollar, p. 70

Aiken Drum, p. 70

All the Year, p. 71

Ants Go Marching, p. 72

Apple Tree, p. 72

Autumn, p. 72

Beehive, p. 73

Bingo, p. 73

Bow-Wow, p. 73

Chickens, p. 74

Chip, Chop, p. 74

Chubby Little Snowman, p. 74

Clap with Me, One, Two, Three, p. 75

Cobbler and the Mouse, p. 75

Daffy-Down-Dilly, p. 75

Did You Ever See a Lassie?, p. 76

Diddle Diddle Dumpling, p. 76

Doctor Foster Went to Gloucester, p. 76

Donkey, Donkey, p. 77

Down by the Station, p. 77

Elizabeth, Elspeth, Betsey, and Bess, p. 77

Family, p. 78

Farmer Plants the Seeds, p. 78

Farmer Plows the Ground, p. 79

Five Little Kittens, p. 80

Five Little Monkeys, p. 81

Five Plump Peas, p. 81

Five Speckled Frogs, p. 82

Fly Walk, p. 82

Footsteps, p. 82

Friends, p. 83

From Wibbleton to Wobbleton, p. 84

Good Morning, Dear Earth, p. 84

Grandma's Spectacles, p. 84

Hands on Hips, Hands on Knees, p. 85

Head, Shoulders, Knees, and Toes, p. 85

Here We Go 'Round the Mulberry Bush, p. 85

Here's a Ball for Johnny, p. 86

Hey, Diddle Diddle, p. 87

Hickory, Dickory, Dock, p. 87

Home on the Range, p. 88

Hoppity, Hop, p. 88

Hot Cross Buns, p. 88

How Far Is It to Babylon?, p. 89

Humpty Dumpty, p. 89

I Am a Fine Musician, p. 89

I Had a Little Nut Tree, p. 90

I Saw a Ship a-Sailing, p. 90

I See the Moon, p. 90

I'm a Little Teapot, p. 91

I've Been Working on the Railroad, p. 91

If All the World Were Paper, p. 92

If You're Happy and You Know It, p. 92

In the Barn, p. 93

Itsy Bitsy Spider, p. 93

Jack and Jill, p. 94

Jack Be Nimble, p. 94

Jack Sprat, p. 94

Kookaburra, p. 95

Lavender's Blue, p. 95

Little Bird, p. 96

Little Bo-Peep, p. 96

Little Boy Blue, p. 97

Little Ducks, p. 97

Little Jack Horner, p. 98

Little Miss Muffet, p. 99

Little Mousie, p. 99

Little Rabbit, p. 99

Little Robin Redbreast, p. 100

Lucy Locket, p. 100

Mares Eat Oats, p. 100

Mary Had a Little Lamb, p. 101

Minnie and Winnie, p. 101

Mistress Mary, p. 101

My Bonnie Lies over the Ocean, p. 102

My Maid Mary, p. 102

My Turtle, p. 102

Nonsense Round, p. 103

Oats, Peas, Beans, p. 103

Old MacDonald, p. 103

Old Mother Hubbard, p. 103

Once I Caught a Fish Alive, p. 104

One Elephant Went Out to Play, p. 104

One, Two, Buckle My Shoe, p. 105

Open Them Shut Them, p. 105

Over in the Meadow, p. 106

Over the Meadows, p. 107

Owl, p. 108

Oysters, p. 108

Pat-a-Cake, Pat-a-Cake, p. 108

Peas, p. 108

Peas Porridge Hot, p. 109

Pop Goes the Weasel, p. 109

Rock-a-Bye, Baby, p. 109

Rumble, Blunder, p. 110

Rumbling and Rattling, p. 110

She'll Be Coming 'Round the Mountain, p. 110

Simple Simon, p. 111

Sippity Sup, p. 111

Six Thin Things, p. 111

Skin-a-ma-rink, p. 112

Skip to My Lou, p. 112

Snail Song, p. 113

Softly, Softly, p. 113

Teddy Bear, p. 113

Ten Little Fingers, p. 113

There Was a Crooked Man, p. 114

This Old Man, p. 114

Three Little Kittens, p. 116

Three Wise Men of Gotham, p. 116

Three Young Rats, p. 116

Tom, Tom, the Piper's Son, p. 117

Twinkle, Twinkle, Little Star, p. 117

Two Apples, p. 117

Two Little Blackbirds, p. 118

Two Little Hands, p. 118

Vintery, Mintery, Cutery, Corn, p. 118

Wheels on the Bus, p. 119

Whirling Leaves, p. 119

Wiggling and Jiggling, p. 120

Wind, p. 120

Wise Old Owl, p. 120

Poems

Maud Keary (from *Enchanted Tulips and Other Verses for Children*)

The Alphabet, p. 121

A Beetle Tale, p. 121

A Dream, p. 122

A Fly, p. 122

A Snail, p. 123

At Night, p. 123

Beneath the Sea, p. 123

Birthdays, p. 123

Blackberries, p. 124

Clouds, p. 124

Cuckoo Flowers and Daisies, p. 124

Enchanted Tulips, p. 125

Fairyland, p. 125

Stand Still and Watch, p. 126

The Steam Engine, p. 126

In the Field, p. 126

In the Wood, p. 127

Jack Frost, p. 127

The Moon, p. 128

My Father Is Extremely Tall, p. 129

My Fingers, p. 129

The Oak, p. 130

Pretty Mouse, p. 130

The Primrose, p. 131

The Rainbow, p. 131

The Wind, 132

The Raindrops, p. 132

Responsibility, p. 132

River, River, p. 132

The Sailor, p. 133

The Shepherd Boy, p. 133

The Snow Queen, p. 133

Swinging, p. 134

The Windmill, p. 134

To a Bee, p. 134

When the Great Wind, p. 134

Who Blows You Out?, p. 135

Who Is That Singing?, p. 135

Wildflowers, p. 135

Wishes, p. 136

Edward Lear (from *A Book of Nonsense*)

Assorted limericks, p. 136

Dollie Radford (from *The Young Gardeners' Kalendar*)

January, p. 140

February, p. 140

March, p. 141

April, p. 142

May, p. 142

June, p. 143

July, p. 144

August, p. 144

September, p. 145

October, p. 145

November, p. 146

December, p. 146

Robert Louis Stevenson (from *A Child's Garden of Verses*)

At the Sea Side, p. 147

Bed in Summer, p. 147

Block City, p. 147

The Cow, p. 148

Fairy Bread, p. 149

The Flowers, p. 149

Foreign Lands, p. 150

Happy Thoughts, p. 150

The Land of Nod, p. 150

The Little Land, p. 151

My Kingdom, p. 153

My Shadow, p. 154

Nest Eggs, p. 154

Rain, p. 155

Singing, p. 155

The Sun's Travels, p. 156

The Swing, p. 156

Time to Rise, p. 156

To Any Reader, p. 157

Where Go the Boats, p. 157

The Wind, p. 158

Windy Nights, p. 158

Verses and Poems Especially for Grade 3

Am I, p. 159

Autumn Color, p. 159

Building a House, p. 159

Cow Talk, p. 160

Farewell Summer, p. 161

Farmer, p. 161

Go with Me, p. 162

In March, p. 162

Jangling Jam Jars, p. 163

Mighty Smith, p. 163

My Heart, p. 163

November Comes, p. 164

The Pasture, p. 164

Punctuation Matters, p. 164

Seeing Ghosts, p. 165

Stopping by Woods on a Snowy Evening, p. 165

Sugar Camp, p. 165

Two Hands We Have, p. 166

The Village Blacksmith, p. 167

We Do, p. 168

When I Wake, p. 168

Winken, Blinken, and Nod, p. 169